REMOTE WORKS

REMOTE WORKS

MANAGING FOR FREEDOM, FLEXIBILITY, AND FOCUS

ALI GREENE AND TAMARA SANDERSON

Berrett–Koehler Publishers, Inc.

Berrett-Koehler Publishers, Inc.
1333 Broadway, Suite 1000
Oakland, CA 94612-1921
Tel: (510) 817-2277; Fax: (510) 817-2278
www.bkconnection.com

ORDERING INFORMATION

Quantity sales. Special discounts are available on quantity purchases by corporations, associations, and others. For details, contact the "Special Sales Department" at the Berrett-Koehler address above.

Individual sales. Berrett-Koehler publications are available through most bookstores. They can also be ordered directly from Berrett-Koehler: Tel: (800) 929-2929; Fax: (802) 864-7626; www.bkconnection.com.

Orders for college textbook/course adoption use. Please contact Berrett-Koehler: Tel: (800) 929-2929; Fax: (802) 864-7626.

Distributed to the U.S. trade and internationally by Penguin Random House Publisher Services.

Berrett-Koehler and the BK logo are registered trademarks of Berrett-Koehler Publishers, Inc.

Printed in Canada

Berrett-Koehler books are printed on long-lasting acid-free paper. When it is available, we choose paper that has been manufactured by environmentally responsible processes. These may include using trees grown in sustainable forests, incorporating recycled paper, minimizing chlorine in bleaching, or recycling the energy produced at the paper mill.

Library of Congress Cataloging-in-Publication Data
Names: Greene, Ali, author. | Sanderson, Tamara, author.
Title: Remote works : managing for freedom, flexibility, and focus / Ali Greene and Tamara Sanderson.
Description: First edition. | Oakland, CA : Berrett-Koehler Publishers, [2023] | Includes bibliographical references and index.
Identifiers: LCCN 2022024893 (print) | LCCN 2022024894 (ebook) | ISBN 9781523003310 (paperback ; alk. paper) | ISBN 9781523003327 (pdf) | ISBN 9781523003334 (epub) | ISBN 9781523003341
Subjects: LCSH: Virtual work teams—United States. | Communication in Management—United States. | Organizational change—United States.
Classification: LCC HD66 .G735 2023 (print) | LCC HD66 (ebook) | DDC 658.4/022—dc23/eng/20220610
LC record available at https://lccn.loc.gov/2022024893
LC ebook record available at https://lccn.loc.gov/2022024894

First Edition
30 29 28 27 26 25 24 23 22   10 9 8 7 6 5 4 3 2 1

Book production: Linda Jupiter Productions; *Edit:* Elissa Rabellino; *Text design:* Kim Scott, Bumpy Design; *Proofread:* Susan Gall; *Cover design:* Ashley Ingram; *Index:* Lieser Indexing; *Tamara Sanderson photo:* Lindsay Davenport; *Figure 1.1:* Top: ©iStock/cyano66; Bottom: ©iStock/Ross Helen

Thank you laptop warriors and email curators.
Thank you office traitors.
Thank you "status quo" instigators.
Thank you nine-to-five meddlers.
Thank you digital nomads here and there.
Thank you remote workers everywhere.

Thank you passenger seat of my car.
Thank you homes near and far.
Thank you library and coffee shop.
Thank you patio, sofa, and desktop.
Thank you airport lounge and your comfy chair.
Thank you to coworking spaces everywhere.

The end. (We're kidding—this is just the beginning.)

Contents

Foreword

WHEN I ENVISIONED the distributed work revolution, it wasn't due to a global pandemic. And while the circumstances that led us here are terrible, I'm glad that we're rethinking how we work.

The illusion that the office is about work has been shattered forever, and companies that embrace remote work will be better positioned to withstand the test of time. If we've learned anything from the pandemic, it's that we can never be sure about what tomorrow will bring.

The thing is, remote work isn't new. But with change, things often happen slowly and then all at once. The forces that enable working in a distributed fashion have been in motion for decades, and if you talk to anyone who was working in technology in the '60s and '70s, they expected this to happen much sooner. Stephen Wolfram has been a remote CEO for 30 years. Automattic has been distributed-first since our founding in 2005.

What's been holding companies back is fear of the unknown and attachment to the familiar. I can't tell you how many of the CEOs who said this would never work for them are now proclaiming that their company hasn't missed a beat as tens of thousands of people started working from home during the COVID-19 pandemic. And the investors I see espousing distributed work are the same ones who once told me that Automattic would never scale past a few dozen people unless we brought everyone into an office.

For this to really work, distributed work has to be part of the company's DNA. You have to be committed to keeping the creative center and soul of the organization online, and not in an office. At Automattic, we use the term *distributed* because to be "remote" suggests there's an office somewhere that you're not part of—it feels isolating.

· · · · · ·

When I founded Automattic, a software company that started with WordPress.com and has expanded to a full suite of other tools and brands, I wanted to give people a benefit above and beyond what others ever could: We gave people the perk and the luxury of being part of an internet-changing company from anywhere in the world. We treat people on the basis of the quality of their ideas and their work, regardless of whether they're in San Francisco or Buenos Aires.

Our work at Automattic is far from finished, and I hope there are hundreds of failures we learn from over the next 20 years. Half the time I feel like we're making it up as we go along—I've never managed a distributed company of 2,000 people before. But the important things stay the same: the desire for impact and my love for working alongside people in a team, doing more than we ever could alone. For me, this is a life's work.

Where this model can sometimes go wrong is if people don't have a strong network outside of their work—in which case they can become isolated and fall into bad habits. Doing it right requires a redesign of your life. For decades, we've built our lives around work, and now we have the opportunity to build our work around our lives. But it takes time, and it takes intentionality. I encourage you to join groups, play sports, and get out into your community. And if you've done all of this and you still haven't found your niche, start your own.

As a fun example, a few years back we had 14 employees in Seattle who wanted to beat the isolation by meeting up for work once a week. They found a local bar that didn't open until 5 p.m., pooled together the $250 per month coworking stipends that Automattic provides, and persuaded the bar's owner to let them rent out the place during the daytime.

This is just one example, but there's an overarching lesson here that applies to any manager. You have to trust the people you've hired. That's when the magic of remote work happens. You start believing in one another's autonomy to get the work done, and then you witness the results when you give people the freedom to truly act upon their abilities, their creative capacity, and their ideas. Fundamentally, remote work only *works* when you release control.

I consider remote work a moral imperative. It's far more humane for workers. The micro-interactions of the hundreds of variables of your work environment can charge you and give you creative energy, or make you dependent, infantilized, and a character in someone else's story. Which do you want to spend half of your waking, workday hours in?

But it's not just an individual company story. Distributed work evens the playing ground worldwide.

No longer are people beholden to the lottery of birth. At Automattic, we have employees located in 96 countries speaking 120 languages. You get a unique richness from accessing a global talent pool, which creates better products but also spreads economic opportunity more widely than it has been in the past. It also helps you break away from office meeting norms, where the highest-paid person's opinion matters most. When remote work is done well, people have time to sit with an idea and contribute, regardless of where they are based or what role they hold.

Now that, hopefully, you're feeling inspired, I want to turn to the reason we're all here. To make remote work *actually* work for you and your team under the esteemed guidance of Ali and Tamara.

In true remote work style, I first met Tam on Slack during her final round of interviews for Automattic. I asked her what book she would give to all of Automattic and what inscription she would write inside. In some ways, this book is bringing that question full circle, and now I'm the one writing the inscription.

Sometimes there can be an assumption that remote jobs are not quite as "real" as office jobs. But I can assure you that Tam did important work at Automattic. She led the integration of our largest acquisition to date (Tumblr), managed some of our most complicated partnerships, and assisted me with our Series D fundraising. But what I remember most about Tam is her enthusiasm for remote work.

We'd be in meetings with executives, and like clockwork, she'd captivate the audience with stories about the power of remote work, often flying in from somewhere exotic like Tbilisi or Mexico City. She said that remote work had given her a superpower. Gone were the days of hastily typed notes and forgotten handovers before partnership meetings. She was omnipresent and omnipotent because we had a record of every partnership meeting since Automattic's inception documented on P2, our internal blogging platform. Of course, this seems normal to me, but maybe that's just my vantage point.

At Automattic, we are all about practicing what we preach. We use our own software internally and are committed to the power of open-source technology. Therefore, I'm excited that you'll find the same principles in *Remote Works*. Tam and Ali cowrote this book while living on separate continents. Ali comes from a remote work organization I admire, DuckDuckGo, and was their director of People Operations. I know firsthand how hard it is to scale a company, and during Ali's time at DuckDuckGo, she helped grow the company from 30 to nearly 100 employees.

But Ali and Tam didn't stop with their firsthand knowledge. They harnessed the wisdom of crowds, interviewing dozens of experts from incredible remote companies. *Remote Works* uses a learn-by-doing mentality—encouraging you to think, reflect, and act, as they walk you through the steps to making remote work for your team, but also your life.

The truth is, there are a thousand ways to do remote work, but it starts with committing to it at all levels of the company. If you assume positive intent and place trust in your coworkers and employees—knowing that if they do great work in an office they can do great work anywhere—then you will all succeed.

But don't just take my word for it—take what's in this book and try it yourself!

—Matt Mullenweg

Preface

HELLO,

We are so excited that you've picked up this book! Not only because we believe you're on a path to designing the remote work life of your dreams, but also because it contains all of the remote work lessons we've learned firsthand along the way (along with dozens more from our fellow remote work leaders). It is all the advice we wish we had when we first started, and we can't wait to share it with you!

But first, we need you to do one thing: *Drop your remote work baggage at the door.*

We get it. We also have a love-hate relationship with Zoom and have been in countless conversations where eyes glaze over the second we say we're advocates for remote work. The thing is, when we started writing this book, the world was at the height of a global pandemic that looked *nothing* like the remote work we've known and loved. It's been exhausting, even for us. All of this to say . . . *there must be a better way.*

Don't worry; we guarantee you there is. We know it. We have lived it (more on that later).

Remote work is no longer a futuristic pipe dream for a few lucky people. It is the present—whether or not companies are ready to adapt. If you are sending emails, saving data to the cloud, or using countless other forms of technology, you have the tools you need to design the how, where, and when to do your best work. The real challenge lies in changing the human behaviors on your team, yourself included, to have true *remote work fluency*: something we define as having the right skills, behaviors, and mindset to easily navigate work in an anytime, anywhere environment as if it is second nature.

Fundamentally, remote work puts a magnifying glass on all aspects of an organization: the good, the bad, and the ugly. We believe the bad and the ugly are merely areas to improve and problems to solve. While we don't claim to have *all* the answers, we do believe in *you*—a competent, capable, and creative human being.

That's why *Remote Works* leans on reflection questions, expert interviews, group activities, and stories so that you can cocreate the best remote work life for yourself and your team—along with us, chapter by chapter. No special software needed. No complex reorganizational plan required.

Last but not least, we want you to know that we live and breathe what we preach, even beyond our combined two decades spent working in distributed environments at places such as Automattic and DuckDuckGo. The last time we saw each other "in real life," before embarking on this writing journey, was in February 2019 in Mexico City. We were roommates for a month while organizing remote working salons.

The idea for this book came up during a casual catch-up while in lockdown during the COVID-19 pandemic. We saw midlevel managers struggling, and executive teams didn't know how to help, given they were also unfamiliar with remote work. We saw them largely copy and paste traditional ways of working into a virtual environment. And then we got to work.

Our biggest fear was that the promise of remote work would be taken away for future generations of knowledge workers due to failed experimentation before most people even got to experience the true benefits: Seemingly simple benefits like creating our workdays around our natural energy peaks and valleys, and enjoying the freedom of choice in our schedule and locations. Bigger benefits too. Because of remote work, we found our partners, developed meaningful relationships, learned from other cultures, improved our health, and had the opportunity to work with some of the best and brightest people from around the world.

We've spent time teaching people on the fundamental questions you should be asking if you are committed to exploring remote options for your team. Many of those questions are woven throughout these pages. We found that once you start questioning, there is no stopping. With remote work, you open the doors to redefine work-life balance, success, and so much more!

We created this book for you and your team, each writing from our corners of the world. With multiple versions of stories in Google Docs, WhatsApp threads, and Asana tasks, we've strengthened our own remote working muscles as well. (Trust us, there's always room for improvement.) We became even more confident that remote work fluency is here to stay. Strong remote work skills will improve your work game, even if you decide to be colocated part of the time. We are excited to share everything we have learned.

Saddle up. Let's get started.

Ali & Tam

README–
A Guide to *Remote Works*

IT CAN TAKE some people a lifetime, but for Michael Judge, it took less than three months to see through the mirage of corporate life and spot its main culprit: bad management.

After graduating with a degree in physics from the University of California, San Diego, in 1985, Michael headed to the optimistic land of Silicon Valley to work as an engineer at a start-up video card company. It didn't last long. But he did leave with an insight that would one day manifest as a box-office sleeper, turned cult classic, turned cultural milestone—*Office Space*.[1]

The movie hit a chord with the American public—surprising given the mainstream hypothesis that people watch movies to *escape* their mundane lives, not relive them. We believe that *Office Space* gave people a mirror to understand their work lives, including what frustrates them—like the infamous manager popping up unexpectedly in their cubicle (yet again) to ask for that (incredibly unnecessary) TPS report.

So, what does this have to do with *Remote Works*? Isn't this a book for managers and their teams?

OK, please don't put down the book yet! Yes, this is a book about work.

And yes, we believe that management is incredibly important.

We've taken the brief from Michael Judge. Bad management is a *real* problem. We believe there's a better way—and that bad management caused by the shift to remote work can be prevented. We want to help you avoid becoming one of the Bobs!

HOW TO READ *REMOTE WORKS*

There are many ways to interact with *Remote Works*. We present concepts in various ways because we know that each reader learns differently.

Think of us as your asynchronous remote work coaches. We are here to guide you and help you strengthen your remote work muscles. We are *not* here to tell you what to do in a step-by-step guide, expecting you to do everything we say (in the correct order).

We believe *great* remote teams come in all shapes and sizes. Regardless of whether you work at a start-up or the largest multinational organization in the world, these principles stay the same because they are focused on the team level. Ultimately, they require customizing remote work principles to your team's unique personality. Only you know that best.

It is up to you to choose your own adventure. So if you find yourself in chapter 8 thinking to yourself, "Oh no . . . not another table," feel free to skip the table and read one of the real-life stories from our experts instead. (Or go ahead and fill out the table. You may be surprised by what you learn from it.) Whether you prefer learning by doing, learning through others, or learning by self-inquiry, we have you covered!

• • • • • •

Ready to get started? Here is what you can expect while reading *Remote Works*:

1. **TL;DR:** Each chapter starts with a section called TL;DR, which stands for "Too Long; Didn't Read," highlighting three to five skills you will unlock by reading the chapter. Think of this section as an anchor; it can help you navigate the book if you prefer to skip around. Plus, the TL;DR is a remote work best practice for documentation. Whether writing up notes or creating a project plan, the TL;DR is a way to summarize content up front for the audience. They can then choose whether it makes sense to dive into the details. (What can we say? We love to practice what we preach.)

2. **Exercises and How-tos:** You'll find several interactive exercises that you can do solo or with your team. Anytime you see an exercise starting with "RW" (shorthand for *Remote Works*), it's something we've created especially for you. You can do the exercises directly in the book (grab a pen!) or access more online resources at remoteworksbook.com.

3. **Spotlight Stories and Experts:** We interviewed more than 30 remote work leaders about their experiences. We highlight their stories as "spotlights" throughout the book. You can learn from others by seeing how they've approached similar situations. Since we frequently quote and share stories from our experts, we give their name and occasionally their company. You can find a complete list of our remote work leaders at the back of the book in the "Experts" section.

4. **Reflection Questions:** After each concept, you'll find reflection questions to help you apply the learnings to your work life. We recommend that you continue to muse over them, perhaps on a long walk or during a shower. (Come on, this is where

we all do our best thinking. Warning, though: the book is not waterproof!)

5. **Ali's Advice and Tam's Tips:** We end each chapter with a bit of real talk, where we share direct, no-filter advice for becoming a pro remote manager and teammate. It's what we *wish* we'd known before we started managing remote teams and projects.

6. **Glossary:** We reference tools and companies across the book, which we *know* may change over time. Rather than explaining these in depth in the chapters, we've created a glossary at the back of the book.

7. **RW Journeys:** Sometimes, learning together can be more fun. Therefore, we've developed an RW Journeys guide to facilitate small groups reading, reflecting, and learning together. We recommend this for learning and development and human resources teams as an alternative approach to management training.

8. **RW Student Case Study:** *Remote Works* can bring a fresh voice to the classroom. Professors can use our book as a part of their curriculum and assign the case study as practice.

• • • • • •

OK, that's a long list! We know we threw a lot at you, but there is one thing to remember: this is a book we hope you continue to refer back to, time and time again.

SEEING YOURSELF AS A REMOTE MANAGER

As we mentioned at the beginning of this chapter, *Remote Works* is focused on you: the manager.

First things first. Let's define *manager* because you likely already have a definition.

Traditionally, a manager ensured that others complied with the when, where, and how of working. These traditional managers usually had functional expertise, like finance or sales, and were given a host of people responsibilities, like delegating tasks, mentoring, and providing performance feedback.

But remote has changed all of that. Now that employees are distributed and have more control over their workflow, it no longer makes sense to have one type of manager. Many of the jobs previously on the manager's plate, such as delegating and reporting to other stakeholders, can be replaced by remote best practices, such as documentation, asynchronous updates, and a culture of transparency.

In remote, *we all become managers*, at least over our workflow and environment. Remote requires a new level of autonomy and mastery, which we will discuss later.

As we reflected on our remote experience and that of other remote companies, we found that management roles in remote include four different personas: the People Manager, the Project Manager, the Cultural Leader, and the Strategic Leader.

The *People Manager* is likely the most similar to the traditional manager but takes on a more relational role in remote. You ensure that each team member realizes their human potential at work and can successfully navigate the organization.

The *Project Manager* plans out the dependencies and milestones for projects and processes. You know what needs to happen to keep tasks moving and can help unblock obstacles when a project gets stuck. We believe that *every* remote worker needs to be a skilled project manager.

The *Cultural Leader* leaves a mark on the organization. You champion team norms, promote cultural events and rituals, and help others connect their work to the organization's goals and mission.

Lastly, the *Strategic Leader* challenges internal thought processes, prioritizes team objectives, and makes sure you're using the tools effectively to reach your team's goals.

The roles and responsibilities of a traditional manager are spread across multiple personas in remote, creating a network effect. Rather than going to one manager for all your work needs, you'll build relationships with multiple people, creating a deep sense of connection in a virtual environment. For example, you might go to one manager for professional development and another for feedback on a project.

Ultimately, everyone has multiple managers and becomes some type of manager persona.

Tamara, aka Tam, most often filled the role of a Project Manager or Strategic Leader during her career, managing complex partnerships, deal processes, and acquisition integrations. Earlier in her career, Tam loved playing the part of a Cultural Leader, organizing social events and inviting speakers to join team meetings. (Once upon a time, she was referred to as "very Google-y.")

Ali steered organizations as a Cultural Leader and Project Manager, developing managerial skills in others and building community. As the companies she worked for grew and changed, so did her role. At DuckDuckGo, this meant shifting into a Strategic Leader role to up-level their People Operations department[2] while managing five internationally distributed teammates as their People Manager.

Enough about us. What's most important is that you start seeing yourself as a manager in your organization. We hope you can immediately apply the lessons from *Remote Works*—whether you're managing a single project or a team of two, 225, or an entire organization!

❓ REFLECTION QUESTIONS

1. What have you gained from remote work? What has your team gained?

2. What are three ways you can celebrate the benefits of remote work?

3. What might be missing in your approach to remote work? What is your team missing?

4. What are three ways you can fill those gaps remotely?

A CAVEAT ON "REMOTE" MANAGEMENT

One last housekeeping item before diving into the good stuff. We assume you picked up this book expecting to learn about remote work (and we promise you will). But as a warning, it will cover *more* than just best practices for remote and hybrid. We believe remote fluency will be a requirement for any job in the future. Regardless of whether you're managing a fully distributed team or simply want to give your team more flexibility and keep the office, the same core skills apply. (Though, we would be liars if we didn't state our personal preference that offices should be optional.)

Some of the management best practices we cover may sound familiar—because they are evergreen. We've taken the wisdom of management best practices from "the before times" and reimagined them for the remote world. You'll learn how to apply motivation theory and usher your team through the phases of team development.

Ultimately, remote work puts a microscope on your management abilities. You have to be more intentional. You can't expect your team to be waiting nearby for eight or nine hours per day if you have a last-minute request. You can't forget to agree on deliverables and timelines because you can rely on a quick check-in by the coffee machine. You need to not only plan but consider others in your plans. Your words and actions have consequences.

Otherwise, you're leaving the benefits of remote work on the conference room table—such as true flexibility, freedom, and focus.

So before you read any further, we want to highlight a few core beliefs that we believe are nonnegotiable for making remote work actually work.

1. Managers must lead with intentionality.

2. Managers must build trust.

3. Managers must respect employees' autonomy.

If you believe in those principles but your organization does not, you'll fight an uphill battle. If you don't believe in those principles, you might as well throw this book out the window or kindly gift it to someone who cares.

Enough with the warnings. Let's build our remote management skills!

💬 ALI'S ADVICE

The business world has been using *manager* and *leader* all wrong! It's time to unlearn the definitions you grew up hearing and challenge the shared vocabulary at your company. A single person cannot do it all, and there is no one way to be a manager. Be honest with yourself about your responsibilities, your influence, and how you can inspire your team.

Challenging assumptions is key to a remote state of mind, which we'll cover in the next chapter. Once you question one thing, you can question nearly everything. The redesign is where things get fun!

You can use this book to change your work and your life. As you read, think through the skills, knowledge, and steps required to design a successful remote work team.

🙂 TAM'S TIPS

The poet E. E. Cummings once published an article of encouragement and counseling in a small Michigan newspaper, and I believe his wisdom applies to remote work: "To be nobody-but-yourself—in a world which is doing its best, night and day, to make you everybody else—means to fight the hardest battle which any human being can fight."[3]

Remote work gives you the freedom and flexibility to design a life that fits you. No longer are you subjected to the winds and influence of a nine-to-five traditional work culture.

Take this as an opportunity to ask tough questions and rethink what it means to manage and be a professional. No one else is going to do it for you. (But we'll be there to help.)

CHAPTER ONE

Remote State of Mind

🎯 TL;DR

In this chapter, we will define what it means to have a remote state of mind and explore the cultural shift to remote using the 5Ws and 1H framework (Who, What, When, Where, Why, How).

At the end of it, you'll be able to do the following:

✓ Question your assumptions in order to create a more fulfilling workplace culture by embracing remote work.

✓ Embrace the true benefits of remote work, such as hiring the best people globally and having more freedom and flexibility while still producing high-quality work.

LET'S START BY playing a game. Take a look at the two photos in figure 1.1. What differences do you see?

Telecommuting entered the public interest in the 1990s after Microsoft launched Microsoft Office (remember Clippy?). The advent of the personal computer inspired a wave of digital enthusiasts, dreamers, and dot-com entrepreneurs (at least until the bust), who imagined a different future.

As Woody Leonhard, a 1990s blogger and author of those bright yellow *Windows for Dummies* books, once said, "Work is something you do, not something you travel to."[1] This is truer than ever today.

Since then, this utopian dream of being able to work from anywhere, at any time, without the grating aspects of office life—commuting, micromanagement, bleak office parks, smelly lunches, loud

FIGURE 1.1 Comparison of Work, Then and Now

talkers—has moved in fits and starts. Behavior is notoriously hard to change—hence, all the gym memberships purchased in January that grow dormant by March. Our habitual nature is partially why remote work has stayed on the fringes despite the technical capabilities being in place.

Sure, there had been hype around digital nomadism and beachfront coworking hubs on Instagram (no complaints here—we would be lying if we said there was no photo evidence of us working at a beachfront café). But the real mass movement to remote working happened in 2020 when COVID-19 turned the world upside down. Knowledge workers and their organizations were slingshot into the future with little preparation and lots of panic. There were Band-Aid solutions and emergency transition plans. And then back-to-office plans, later reneged as the pandemic carried on. We'll remember the early 2020s as the years we survived by adapting to remote work.

But before we potentially send you down the memory lane of rough patches with remote work, we want to remind you that you likely practiced some form of remote working even *before the pandemic.*

It was a common theme as we interviewed remote work experts across the globe, and upon reflection, it applied to us as well!

Let's take a look at their stories for inspiration. You may find you've already been flexing your remote muscles too.

REMOTE ORIGIN STORIES

The Frequent Flier

Tam Sanderson (yes, one of the two names on the cover) decided there must be a better way after spending her first year as a management consultant flying to and from Dallas in 2006. She ended her lease on her uptown apartment in 2007, where she rarely was, and started living in hotels near her consulting projects (and with friends and family when back in the United States). Her "homes" were the Sheraton hotel in El Salvador and the Four Points in Zurich; she bopped between London and Dublin (cue the movie *Up in the Air*, except there was no George Clooney), exploring bits of Europe and North Africa in between.

She didn't realize she was working remotely, even though she was flying back to her home office only once a quarter. All she needed were her BlackBerry and laptop computer. While she had yet to learn the art of traveling lightly (she kept two rolling suitcases in the luggage check at her hotel), she had opened her eyes to a fundamental truth: in many cases, you can untether your work from your location.

The Freelancer

While *freelancer* is often associated with the digital nomad, we found in our conversations that many freelancers started working remotely out of necessity.

For example, Staszek Kolarzowski, cofounder of Pilot, a payroll and benefits platform, was hired by a local marketing agency in Poland to make digital animations. But there was one problem. Staszek was still in high school. "I had to go to lessons. I couldn't go to the office. So, we had an agreement. I was the only person on the team who could work flexible hours and from home. I met them in person every few months because we were in the same city, but besides that, I worked from home. It was great! Super-flexible. They only cared about deadlines, so I could organize myself and work from my hub."

Likewise, Andrew Gobran of Doist found himself freelancing in college. "I designed Prezis for people all over the world. At the time, I never thought, 'Oh, this is a remote role.' But I developed many skills, like communication across cultures and time zones, managing individual autonomy, and having responsibilities and owning them."

The Colocated

On the other hand, some found themselves technically remote working . . . in an office. For example, Ali Greene (Hi! Yes, the other coauthor) started her career at the fast-growing start-up LivingSocial, at the height of the group-coupon craze. When she first started, the company easily fit into a small office in Chinatown in Washington, DC. But they quickly grew out of that office and expanded to a second office across the street. Soon, they had offices in different neighborhoods of DC and had local salespeople based on the ground in the United States and Canada.

Ali soon found that meetings previously conducted around a conference table were now being scheduled as conference calls; likewise, information was being shared via systems like Salesforce and not by shouting across the cramped shared desks, as in her early days.

Sara Robertson, of Edinburgh Futures Institute, noticed something similar while working at a software company early in her career. "They were using Jira and GitLab. They were all in the same room, but they hardly ever spoke to each other, which was a completely new experience in an office for me. Sometimes they would decide to work from home for the day. And it didn't affect anything."

The same was true for Daniel Davis, formerly of DuckDuckGo, when he was working at Opera in Japan. He found that although colocated, they were all working on different things. "Nobody knew what I was working on. It was similar to being in a shared office where you don't talk about your work because you don't know what everyone's work is. Instead, you talk about movies and games."

Whether you've been a remote worker since high school or first prototyped a new way of working during the COVID-19 pandemic, we can sense that something is different. It can sometimes feel intangible, and we know that it's more than just videoconferences. It's truly a state of mind.

❓ REFLECTION QUESTIONS

1. When in your career have you flexed your "remote work fluency" muscles—regardless of whether you were fully remote, sometimes remote, or working in an office?

2. What did you like and dislike about the remote work experience?

3. How could you improve that situation today with the right tools and policies?

THE PATH TO THE FUTURE

Before you embark on your remote working journey, you need a remote state of mind. What's that? It differs for everyone, but it ultimately comes down to a few things.

First and foremost, it's the ability to conduct your job remotely. Today, this means harnessing the power of the internet so that your workflows, information, and processes are saved on the cloud and accessible anywhere. Though we'd argue you can still be a remote worker with just a phone.

Once you've covered the work, it is time for a mindset shift. You begin asking questions (like *where* and *when* you do your best work), challenging the status quo (that commuting is normal), and imagining your ideal work life (if you had more variables in your control).

Does that sound like a tall order? We're here to help. This chapter will explore how to get you into a remote state of mind using the journalistic framework—5Ws and 1H (Who, What, When, Where, Why, How).

The *Who*

You are no longer limited to teammates in the same room or even the same country. You have the opportunity to hire the best team from all over the globe and leverage time zone differences to create an around-the-clock workforce if needed.

You've probably heard the phrases "The future is here; it is just not evenly distributed" or "the lottery of birth." Remote work can level the playing field and give more people access to opportunities, regardless of their zip code or passport.

Even if your team stays the same, the way you get to know them and collaborate with them has changed. You can no longer rely on hallway conversations or elevator rides for small talk. You may recognize coworkers' avatars now more than their body language. As a manager or a teammate, you need to shift your relationship-building methods and find new ways to learn about each other—perhaps using the backgrounds on their video screen as a head start.

You'll also need to rethink your daily socialization. Gallup polls used to say that having a friend at work increased job satisfaction.[2] While it is important to have strong relationships and trust in your team, we believe that in a remote world, sometimes you just need a friend *to work with* and not necessarily at your same company, whether at a café, in your backyard, or at the office. You can also intermix socialization breaks, either virtually or in real life, between focus time or meetings. Ali often coworks with her partner from their kitchen table and with family members, joking that her sister's house turned into the "Family HQ" for work during her last visit home. Tam also recommends getting involved with your local community if you are new in town, like volunteering, playing sports, taking continuing education classes, and joining Meetup groups.

Remote State of Mind

On staying in your local community . . .

"Not requiring folks to move and enabling them to stay deeply embedded in their life/community allows for less stress and greater satisfaction." —ANNE McCARTHY

On opening up your hiring pool . . .

"If you are looking to recruit in one kind of location or a handful of locations, you have significantly closed up your diversity pool to people who live within commutable distance to that office. Many socioeconomic factors have determined your talent pool." —**HILARY CALLAGHAN**

On expanding opportunity . . .

"Why does the accident of birth have to determine their life path? Remote work is completely deconstructing this." —**LORRAINE CHARLES**

The *What*

Remember all those ways we used to fill time during the nine-to-five? Meetings to plan meetings. Surfing the internet in a cubicle. Filling out reports that should be automated. Joining meetings that shouldn't be on your calendar (but you were added out of courtesy). Asking, yet again, for a status update.

These things no longer need to exist in a perfect remote world (though they are still happening or you wouldn't be reading this book!). If anything, all the optics of traditional office work can feel more draining when you see the alternatives in front of you, whether it's your child who's just finished school, an offer to meet friends for lunch, or the sun begging you to take a quick stroll.

In traditional office culture, we often conflate things that look like work—how many meetings you attend, how long you were at your desk, face time with your manager at the coffee machine—with real work. When remote work is effective, it focuses less on visual cues and inputs and relies more on measuring the outputs. As mentioned, you were probably doing some remote working already, even if from your office desk. Sending emails, setting up conference calls, working from home on a sick day. Those are all, technically, activities of remote work.

Remote State of Mind

On monitoring results . . .

"At the end of the day, you need to make sure that results are delivered: x is shipped, tickets are closed, or articles are written. Results are more important than whether or not people are sitting at their desks."
—STEPH YIU

On the false god of proximity . . .

"So a lot of management has been by proximity rather than performance. Most of the work is organized around physicality. It's even in our tech systems. We have files. We have a desktop. We have a trash bin. It mimics a physical desk. So much of our paradigms around tech are rooted in a physical sense." —BEN BROOKS

The *When*

Imagine the following scene. It's 26 degrees Celsius outside (79 degrees Fahrenheit for our American friends), not too hot and not too cold. Goldilocks perfect. The sun is shining, the sky is a crayon-box shade of blue, and it's the first day of a local art exhibition you've been dying to see.

But there's one problem—it's a Thursday. In a traditional workplace, you'd witness those perfect clouds from the window of your office building. You might not even have a view because your windows face a parking lot. Or worse, you may work in an office or a cubicle with no window at all! In between meetings, you might try to reserve a weekend ticket online—but you hate crowds, and you're sure that's when everyone else will be trying to see it too. Ali swears by this trick and often reverses her week. She loves to work on weekends and go hiking or out to restaurants on weekdays for this exact reason.

Now, let's cut to the remote world. The "when" matters less if you've coordinated with your team and can finish your work independently. This means you could enjoy that sunny day and the art exhibition for a few hours in the afternoon and complete your tasks that evening. Or you could run an errand for an elderly parent nearby, pick up a sick kid at school, or have that cavity worked on pronto without making a massive production out of it.

By taking advantage of time zones and asynchronous communication, teams can design work schedules around the moments that matter to them, giving them the flexibility they crave.

If you've ever had someone break your trust at work, you might be rolling your eyes now ("Sure, that sounds great, if you live in a utopia"). You don't have to take our word for it. Remote work isn't successful if it's the spitting image of a traditional office on a 13-inch screen. It works when it frees up your time and energy to do your best work while managing your home life with care and creativity.

Remote State of Mind

On making your dream life a reality . . .

"I think the one thing I would say is I would have the leaders of those companies ask themselves, what does their dream life look like? I would ask them to look at their [work] practices and say, 'How could we create a work environment in which many different individuals' dreams can be achieved?'" —**DARCY BOLES**

On breaking out of the nine-to-five routine . . .

"You'd be surprised how many people still do the nine-to-five even when working remotely. I don't understand it. I prefer variety in my day as opposed to routine. As a father of a 20-month-old, I prefer maximizing daylight hours for exercising and being outdoors with my family. Some of my biggest breakthroughs have come to me while trail running (never sitting in an office). My schedule looks different every day, depending on my life/work circumstances." —**CARLOS SILVA**

On the many variations of "perfect" . . .

"What perfect conditions are for 20 people in a team is going to lead to 20 different definitions. By design, you'll always fail. But instead, ask how we empower each individual. Change the organization by activating the individuals, rather than changing the culture or cascading something down. None of those paradigms have worked." —**BEN BROOKS**

On surprising choices . . .

"We let people back to the office on a strictly voluntary basis. And guess what? The day with the highest footfall in the company's headquarters in Mumbai was Friday. Exactly the opposite of what I'd expect in the US. Commuting is so bad, they want to work from home or a nearby coworking center during the week. But they come in on Fridays to socialize and then go out together after work."
—**JASON MORWICK**

The *Where*

The "where" is the most apparent change. You no longer have to commute to the office in rush hour to stay in the same place for eight hours. (Did you know the average worker pre-pandemic spent 4.5 hours per week commuting?)[3]

At a minimum, this means you can design a space customized to you—maybe that's creating a dream home office, picking out a few cafés to add to your rotation, or finding a fun coworking space or public library (like Tam!). On a larger scale, if you're moving to remote full-time, you may relocate closer to family or somewhere less expensive. Or, simply, somewhere you like better.

While hybrid is not something we'll specifically cover in this book, we believe our advice still stands, regardless of location. Ali often says, "If one employee is remote, then the whole company is working remotely." That is to say: the culture, collaboration, documentation, and business operations are remote-first (or should be!). *Hybrid*, therefore, describes a real estate strategy, like deciding whether a company should own or lease private office space in which employees will work. In the future, we believe the lines we draw today—in person, remote, or hybrid—will blur, and all knowledge work will be digital-first.

Remote State of Mind

On headquarters bias . . .

"When I joined the international start-up, they had three primary offices and one headquarters. And the headquarters was where their leadership was. If you were a product manager, you felt like you needed to be there to be in the mix for the decision-making, to be aware of what was happening. Essentially all of their senior leaders relocated to the headquarters . . . hallway conversations were happening all the time. And sometimes those hallway conversations were decision-making conversations on strategy."—**ALI BRANDT**

On location independence . . .

"I left [that job] and sought out somewhere that would give me location independence. So again, I took a big step back financially and in terms of hierarchy within an organization. I joined Doist with one criterion: give me location independence and let me live where I want. . . . I've been now with the company for six years." —**CHASE WARRINGTON**

On keeping remote "a secret" . . .

"I went to India in 2009, for about two to three months, and kept doing my consulting projects. They did not know where I was. It felt back then like a secret I needed to keep. If there was a call they needed to have at 3 EST, I had to wake up in the middle of the night to make that call. That rarely happened, but I did have to do that a couple of times. The idea to keep it secret was probably my insecurity." —**AKSHAY KAPUR**

On having a room of one's own . . .

"Neurodiversity and disabilities take a lot of energy to manage. Getting ready in uncomfortable clothes, leaving the house, driving/taking transportation, and having unnecessary social interactions would be too much. Instead, I can wear comfortable clothes. I can control things like temperature, pets, music, and lights in my workspace, which eliminates a sensory overload." —**CAT CONTILLO**

The *Why*

Transitions are a natural point for reflection. It's so easy to get tied to the day-to-day routine and forget to ask the simple question: Why?

> *Why does your team exist?*

> *Why does a manager exist in your organization?*

> *Why do you want to make "remote" work—for yourself and your team?*

· · · · · ·

Those questions sound deceptively simple. Of course, we should all know why we were hired and what we've been doing five days a week. But in reality, why can be very hard to answer. Luckily, there's no correct answer, and sometimes it even leads to more questions. Like a little kid testing a parent's patience, "Why?" and "Why?" again.

We believe it's through questions, not always answers, that you uncover the root of an issue and find creative solutions to achieve your goals. After all, it is a lesson in intentionality that we see leading the charge of remote work.

Remote State of Mind

On finding your North Star . . .

"Stop for a second and think: What am I really monitoring to ensure that my team is high performing? What is the North Star for this team? How do I make sure that that's highly visible to me, my team, and my boss? That's very powerful. Most managers can't tell you: Why does my team exist? Why does the company pay me? What are the metrics I need to track? How are we performing? You'd be surprised at how many managers don't." —**STEPH YIU**

On finding your superpower . . .

"Honestly, none of my ideas are like 'my ideas.' My first title was chief curator because I was the CEO of $1. I chose chief curator because I'm really listening to great ideas and trying to curate them in a useful way that's practical. My skill is taking amazing ideas and distilling them into actionable ways that you can apply them." —**SALLY THORNTON**

On creating your best life with your family . . .

> "I've spent the last eight years living nomadically and traveling the globe with my wife and two kids. Not only is Hotjar the best job I've ever had, but it's allowed me to also pursue my passion for travel along the way." —KEN WEARY

The *How*

We're sure you've already picked up at least a few tricks on how to make remote work more attractive—whether it's adding a fun background to Zoom or buying an ergonomic chair for your home office. Search online or check out your LinkedIn feed. We're positive you'll find dozens of listicles.[4] We've read a lot of them, and yeah, we wrote a few ourselves.

While those are important, true expertise in remote work requires going deeper to the roots of work to reimagine it. We'll examine the mental models you and your team already have on how work should work. We hope to distill the myth from the truth (what actually needs to happen) and help you better communicate ideas, preserve organizational intellectual capital, and structure workloads.

As Matt Mullenweg, the CEO of Automattic (WordPress.com) and an avid remote work advocate, once blogged, there are essentially "Five Levels of Autonomy" for distributed work.[5] Level zero starts with jobs that *cannot* be done unless you're physically there—for example, nannying an infant, building a house, or working in an end-of-life nursing facility.

As levels of autonomy increase, the efficacy of remote work also increases. By the time an organization reaches level five, work is primarily asynchronous, and the organization is outperforming its doppelgänger in an office. Whether you are on level zero or at moments flying high in remote work Nirvana, we're excited to come along on this journey to help you design remote working experiences for you and your team.

Remote State of Mind

On building trust . . .

"What matters are the outcomes you achieve. So as long as you're achieving the outcomes and delivering your work, it doesn't matter. It is the cornerstone of remote work, isn't it? You've got to have people who you can trust. And you've got self-driven people who understand that they just need to focus on results." **—SIOBHAN MCKEOWN**

On being intentional . . .

"It's not that you cannot do cultural work remotely. Doing it remotely requires you to be more intentional about it. But if you don't intentionally address culture, you're going to have a bad culture in most cases. It's no longer just the atmosphere or an unconscious feeling. It's really about values, processes, and rules on how we interact." **—MARIO GIULIO BERTORELLI**

❓ REFLECTION QUESTIONS

1. Which of the 5Ws and 1H are you most excited by?
2. What's one shift to remote that you (or your teammates) have found challenging?

While the 5Ws and 1H framework is one way to summarize the shifts, we've included a "10 Ways 'Remote' Changed Work" info-graphic for safekeeping (table 1.1). We recommend that you set aside 30 minutes to review the questions in the infographic. You can answer the question prompts alone or with your team.

TABLE 1.1 Infographic—10 Ways "Remote" Changed Work

	THEN	NOW	ASK YOURSELF
1	Geography-dependent recruitment.	Hire the best talent anywhere in the world.	How can you expand your hiring strategy beyond borders?
2	Top jobs in the most expensive cities (New York for banking, San Francisco for tech, Los Angeles for entertainment).	People can choose to work and live anywhere! Geographical coverage and diversity increase.	How will you accommodate team members who work in different time zones?
3	Lots of time commuting—destroying happiness and the environment.	You choose your commute—increasing flexibility and life satisfaction. Better for the environment too.	What will you do with the time you used to spend commuting?
4	Restricted Monday to Friday, nine-to-five schedule.	Flexible hours, work when it's best for you.	When do you do your best work?
5	Face time is valued. Promotes a meeting-based organization.	Output and getting the work done is valued. Balance of meetings and focused work.	How can you communicate and manage outside of a meeting?
6	Focuses on the visibility of inputs (e.g., sending emails, attending meetings, being "busy") and work about work.	Focuses on visibility of outputs (e.g., communicating a project milestone, launching code, closing a deal).	What outputs matter for you and your team?
7	Ideal for managers' schedules (e.g., back-to-back meetings).	Autonomy to balance a maker's schedule and to redefine the manager's schedule.	How can you make time in your calendar for heads-down focus?
8	Ideas were communicated verbally in meetings for those present.	Ideas are shared widely before, after, or in place of meetings, mainly in written form.	How will you facilitate brainstorming and idea generation? Could this be more democratic?
9	Downplays documentation. This leads to a single point of failure when people leave the company.	Documentation is everything! Ideas are captured in writing, more functional and transparent for all.	What tools and processes will you use to document? How will you prevent information overload?
10	Communication through in-office water cooler conversations and through the grapevine.	Intentional communication of ideas through chosen media (e.g., email, Slack).	How will you share important information with your team? How can you increase transparency and visibility?

? REFLECTION QUESTIONS

1. What have you gained from remote work? What has your team gained?

2. What are three ways you can celebrate the benefits of remote work?

3. What might be missing in your approach to remote work? What is your team missing?

4. What are three ways you can fill those gaps remotely?

♥ ALI'S ADVICE

The joy of remote work is that you are reinventing work.

You can learn all the best practices and read all the listicles, but it will mean nothing unless you truly believe in and want your team to thrive in this new iteration of work. It's not about remote versus hybrid versus a return to office. Or about artificial intelligence and robots. It is about integrating best practices into your day-to-day work.

Remote simply adds a magnifying glass to any broken processes, cultural gaps, or miscommunications that already existed in your team. Now you have an opportunity not just to fix it but to make it even better!

☺ TAM'S TIPS

I'm a design thinker with some Buddhist leanings, so my advice would be twofold. First, approach change with curiosity. Ask questions. Be willing to learn and change your mind. Find ways to test new ways of working as a mini-prototype across your organization and then iterate.

Second, let go. Remember, there's only so much in your control. It's great to think and organize and plan, but at some point you have to let nature take its course. Your company will not be the same today as it will be in five years, and it's not the same today as it was five years ago. That's OK.

CHAPTER TWO

Manager Archetypes

🎯 TL;DR

This chapter is all about *you*. We will explore the importance of self-awareness as a remote manager and guide you through a Mad Libs™–inspired exercise and quiz to determine your Manager Archetype. Reflections on your working preferences and habits, as both an individual and a manager, are the highlights of this chapter.

At the end of it, you'll be able to do the following:

✓ Identify how you work best remotely to lead by example and build trust in your team.

✓ Determine your natural management style and develop your ability to flex in various situations.

✓ Adapt to the needs of your team based on how they work in a remote setting.

ONCE UPON A TIME, a 13th-century Persian poet and Sufi mystic, Rumi, wrote a poem about an elephant brought into a village. No one had ever seen an elephant. So, late at night, villagers filed into the dark cave where the elephant was kept and described what they experienced.

The one who touched the trunk described the elephant as "a water-pipe creature." Another who touched its curved back claimed it had a "leathery throne." The proudest of them all, who felt the tusks, was sure that the creature had a "rounded sword made out of porcelain."

While each accurately described an aspect, the perceptions did not add up to the elephant we know and recognize today.

Rumi ended the poem with an insight:

Each of us touches one place
and understands the whole in that way.
The palm and the fingers feeling in the dark
are how the senses explore the reality of the elephant.

If each of us held a candle there,
and if we went in together, we could see it.[1]

You are coming into a team with your perspectives and experience on how work should be done. You know what you've seen and learned, but as Rumi described, it's only a part of the collective experience of "work," let alone remote work.

Instead, you'll want to reflect upon and communicate all that you understand about yourself as a manager—your likes, dislikes, motivations, and more. This act of vulnerability encourages your team to share more about themselves through mirrored actions and open conversations. You'll also build more transparency and honesty to codesign a way of working that accounts for everyone's preferences, strengths, and past experience.

KNOW THYSELF

Tam remembers clearly when her coach at Automattic, Akshay Kapur, challenged her to look inside herself with a simple question: "What do you want?" She faltered on the other end of the Zoom screen, unsure how to answer. And later was disappointed in herself—how could she not know what she wanted? The question led her on a path of self-inquiry.

Tam had spent most of her adult life wandering and moving, which brought a paradox of emotions: exhilarating and humbling, eye-opening and confusing. By her mid-30s, she had adapted to her ever-changing environment so many times that she'd lost some of her own identity.

This adaptation mindset followed her to work, which served a purpose. It was second nature for her to shapeshift into what was needed and help others get what they wanted. She had found a knack for making managing directors successful while she worked diligently behind the scenes, making sure that everything was organized and analyzed just so. But while this skill had its time and place, she had never given the same amount of import to the reverse. What would it look like if her environment adapted to her? What did she want in her career and in life? What were her identities, outside of expat and traveler?

That question from Akshay sent her on a crucial search: to learn more about herself. While she's still doubtful that she'll ever fully know herself (like Carl Jung, she believes individuation is a lifelong process),[2] Tam is confident that she understands herself better now than she did back then. She started building more self-awareness by paying attention to the person she was from when she woke up in the morning to when she went to bed at night. That person who was laughing, playing, scheming, daydreaming, fretting, planning, analyzing, and meaning-making—those were her. By becoming more comfortable with her different modalities, she learned to accept the other parts of herself—the good, the OK, and those nagging bits that she wished were different.

Soon, Tam's life started looking different. She put down roots in Cambridge, Massachusetts, and started getting involved in things she enjoyed and cared about. She signed up for local art classes and volunteered at a food bank. She attended meditation classes and joined a small spiritual group. It became clearer who she was and what she wanted. (This book is a part of that journey.)

It wasn't enough to think about what she wanted and enjoyed. She also started transforming her environment to reflect this new iteration (rather than having her reflect the environment). She filled her apartment with mementos and reminders: tons of books to be read and art that she loved. There are tarot cards, art supplies, and a giant hammock under the elm trees on the balcony. Collectively, they serve as a mirror, reflecting Tam's ever-evolving identity to her.

Like Tam, you will need to reflect on your own needs, wants, and desires before being fully present with your team as a manager. This may be one of the greatest lessons of remote management.

There is little room for managers to honestly know themselves in traditional offices. You show up and leave when everyone else does. You adapt your likes, dislikes, and personality to fit in with those around you and the office environment that someone else designed. You can try to do your best work independently or with others but are often thrown off course by someone else's whims.

In remote work, you can adapt your environment to do your best work, but that requires knowing who you are and what you want. If a traditional office environment has conditioned you, this might be difficult, as it was for Tam.

With general curiosity, start asking yourself questions: What do you want? What do you care about? Who are you when no one is looking? If you're going to lead others, you'll need to become comfortable with yourself first—even the parts you don't like and try your best to hide, ignore, or fix.

✎ EXERCISE: RW Working Style Preferences

In light of Tam's story, you can use the Mad Libs™–inspired exercise that follows to understand who you are as a manager and employee. You no longer need to assimilate into a single archetype of a "good worker" or a "good manager."

We're all coming into a team with past experiences and perspectives. By making them transparent and explicit, you'll shed light on the team's true nature. In the words of Rumi, "If each of us held a candle there, and if we went in together, we could see it."

Instructions

1. Read through the sentences that follow. The sentences in *italics* are meant for manager personas. All team members can answer the rest.

2. Fill in the blanks.

3. Try to complete this in 10 minutes. Don't overthink it! There are no wrong answers. Afterward, we'll reflect on the answers together.

RW Working Style Preferences

On management . . .

➤ I believe that a "good manager" is _____ (ADJ),

_____ (ADJ), and _____ (ADJ).

➤ The best manager I've ever had was _____ (NAME).

I admired his/her/their _____ (NOUN)

because_____

_____ (REASON).

➤ The worst manager I've ever had was _____ (NAME).
There was tension because of _____
_____ (DESCRIPTIVE PHRASE).

➤ *When managing a project, I want contributors to check in by*
_____ (MEDIUM), _____ (FREQUENCY)
to share _____
_____ (DESCRIPTIVE PHRASE).

➤ *When managing a person, I want to communicate with them*
through _____ (MEDIUM), _____ (FREQUENCY)
to share _____
_____ (DESCRIPTIVE PHRASE).

On trust and rapport . . .

➤ I like to build trust by _____
_____ (DESCRIPTIVE PHRASE).

➤ When trust is broken, I need _____
_____ (DESCRIPTIVE PHRASE).

➤ I prefer receiving feedback by _____
_____ (DESCRIPTIVE PHRASE).

On working preferences . . .

➤ I have the most energy for focused work from ____ (HOUR) to
____ (HOUR), during the day.

➤ I need _____

(DESCRIPTIVE PHRASE) in order to get into the zone of focused work.

➤ I have the most energy for virtual meetings from ____ (HOUR) to

____ (HOUR), during the day.

➤ I like meetings that are _____

_____ (DESCRIPTIVE PHRASE).

➤ I need to prepare for meetings by _____

_____ (DESCRIPTIVE PHRASE).

➤ I'm best at communicating when _____

_____ (DESCRIPTIVE PHRASE).

➤ My ideal workspace is _____ (PLACE)

because I like to be surrounded by _____

_____ (DESCRIPTIVE PHRASE)

On ups and downs . . .

➤ I feel **happy** at work when _____

_____ (DESCRIPTIVE PHRASE).

➤ I feel **inspired** at work when _____

_____ (DESCRIPTIVE PHRASE).

➤ I am **surprised or caught off-guard** when _____

_____ (DESCRIPTIVE PHRASE).

➤ I feel **bad** when _____

_____ (DESCRIPTIVE PHRASE).

➤ I feel **angry, stressed, or frustrated** when _____

_____ (DESCRIPTIVE PHRASE).

➤ If I had a magic wand and could change one thing about
work, it'd be _____

_____ (DESCRIPTIVE PHRASE).

On your spot in the universe . . .

➤ My "superpowers" at work are _____

(DESCRIPTIVE PHRASE), _____(DESCRIPTIVE PHRASE), and

_____ (DESCRIPTIVE PHRASE).

➤ If a genie could grant me three wishes, I'd ask for

_____ (NOUN), _____

(NOUN), and _____ (NOUN).

➤ I feel most myself at work or home when I am

_____ (ADJ), _____ (ADJ),

and _____ (ADJ).

➤ *I'd like to be remembered by my team as* _____

_____ (ADJ).

> ### ❓ REFLECTION QUESTIONS
>
> 1. What is one new thing you learned about yourself from the RW Working Style Preferences exercise?
>
> 2. Which of your answers surprised you? Why?
>
> 3. How would you summarize what's important to you at work in one sentence?

FINDING YOUR MANAGER STYLE

Something to know about us is, we love a metaphor, a poem, and a pun—but this time, instead of being highbrow, we'll take it down a notch with an everyday activity: cooking.

Question for you: How many ways are there to cook an egg?

A few come to mind for us—hard-boiled, soft-boiled, scrambled, sunny-side-up, over-easy, poached—but we're sure any brunch lover could add to that list. Regardless of how it's cooked, it's fundamentally an egg.

Think of your manager roles, like People Manager or Project Manager, as the egg. Roles are relatively finite. You are responsible for a project or a team for a set time, and there is a standard set of deliverables and responsibilities that stay the same. You might find that two people have utterly different approaches to people management, but ultimately they are still responsible for supporting employees to accomplish organizational goals.

Styles, however, are more flexible. It's how that egg is cooked. Sometimes, certain situations call for different styles of management. Let's say you want to make a Cobb salad. A hard-boiled egg works better than scrambled. Or perhaps, like Tam, you used to live in Singapore and are craving their famous kaya toast with coconut jam. In that case, a soft-boiled egg is much better than sunny-side up for dipping.

You get the picture. So, before you start getting too hungry, know this: you get to decide how you show up in management.

Let's repeat: you get to decide how you show up in management.

RW Manager Archetypes

It is essential to have a range when it comes to management styles, though you may naturally tend to rely on one style.

When looking into popular theories on leadership, we were inspired by leaders in this space, such as Daniel Goleman, an expert on emotional intelligence who developed the Six Emotional Leadership Styles, and Ken and Margie Blanchard, who created the Situational Leadership model along with Paul Hersey. (We recommend diving further into their work if interested!)

The theories taught us that while you may be a natural at one type of management style, such as being more directive or coaching, you will have to adapt. It's crucial to alter your style to account for the preferences of others and the situation at hand.

As Goleman says, "The best leaders don't know just one style of leadership—they are skilled at several, and have the flexibility to switch between styles as the circumstances dictate."[3]

There are so many factors to play with in remote work. Therefore, it is vital to flex, depending on the managerial scenario, the type of project you're working on, the person you are interacting with, and even the cultural norms of your team members.

Based on our research and lived experiences, we've taken a modern spin on all of our favorite leadership approaches and summarized four primary styles that we've witnessed in remote organizations.

The archetypes we introduce differ based on orientation *toward* the team or away and the level of hands-on involvement in day-to-day tasks. Maybe you are naturally more of an Egg Sheeran than an Egg Zeppelin (a bit of foreshadowing to our next metaphor, music),[4] but it's still important to understand where you "eggist" in the universe of management styles. That way, you can know how you're showing up for your team and whether it aligns with the management style you're striving toward.

So enough with the yolks. Let's get into the RW Manager Archetypes! (We promise that's the last egg pun. Ali just can't help herself.)

Let's walk through the dimensions together (figure 2.1).

Involvement (X-Axis)

- Hands-on involvement describes managers who are more heavily involved in the team's day-to-day activities. It may occur for many reasons: personal preference to be a part of the team, the perception that the team needs support, or sometimes lack of trust.

- Hands-off involvement happens when your team is more self-directed or autonomous. This may occur if you believe your team has a high competence level or a high degree of trust.

FIGURE 2.1 RW Manager Archetypes Matrix

Orientation (Y-Axis)

- Team-focused styles nurture the team's development and ensure that individual members are getting their work needs met. In some cases, these managers may contribute to the team's work (e.g., an engineer who is also a team lead) or play a coaching role.

- Organization-focused styles are concerned with representing their team to the broader organization. This style is excellent at "managing up" and "managing out." They enjoy showcasing the great work of their team to leadership, external partners and customers, or other teams.

✎ EXERCISE: Determining Your RW Manager Archetype

Wondering how you fit into the picture? While your style should flex based on the situation, you can use this quiz to see where you are now or how you most naturally show up.

Hands-On vs. Hands-Off

1. I prefer
   a. to have consistent core working hours for my team and collaborate synchronously.
   b. to have a "work wherever, whenever" policy for my team.

2. I am more likely to
   a. share a goal alongside a straightforward process to reach the goal.
   b. share a goal and let my team create their own strategy for achieving that goal.

3. After a meeting with my team, I usually
   a. prescribe the next steps to the most relevant teammate.

   b. draw out themes and have my team decide how to act on
them.

If you mainly answered *a*'s, you are likely *hands-on*. Mostly *b*'s,
you are likely *hands-off*.

Team- vs. Organization-Focused

1. I tend to spend more of my energy
   a. focused on checking in with how my team is doing and pro-
      tecting my team from external challenges or office politics.
   b. focused on how my team is perceived by the organization
      and ensuring that their performance positively impacts com-
      pany goals.

2. I would rather
   a. be seen as part of the team.
   b. be respected as the team leader.

3. With my team, I mostly talk about
   a. how their strengths contribute to the team, how they want to
      develop, and their personal interests.
   b. the work to be done, how the team can shine within the
      organization, and what is next for the team in terms of com-
      pany priorities.

If you mainly answered *a*'s, you are likely *team-focused*. Mostly
b's, *organization-facing*.

So, where do you fit in?

Circle your answers that follow and find your style using the graphics.

I am   hands-on   hands-off

I am   team-focused   organization-focused

While this quiz is not science, it will help you describe your natural style or where you are today. Remember, certain styles may be more fitting for specific situations.

There will be specific events where your team needs you to march to the beat of a different drum. For example, you may naturally act as a Composer, but when it comes to writing updates for board meetings, you flex to the Promoter, wanting to impress leadership with all the fantastic work that your team's completed.

Let's dive into the RW Manager Archetypes to learn more about each style and the steps you can take to flex into that type when the situation calls for it (figure 2.2).

FIGURE 2.2 Revisiting the RW Manager Archetypes Matrix—Finding Your Style

The Bandleader: Maceo Parker

The Bandleader has something special. Some call it charisma; others see it as easily building trust. Bandleaders are as much a part of the team as they are leaders of the team. They thrive when helping the team build something better together than each individual could contribute on their own, themselves included. Take Maceo Parker as an example.

Maceo Parker is an American treasure. Not only has he performed with nearly every funk leader, calling artists like James Brown and Prince his friends and bandmates, but at the age of 79, he's still performing.

When Tamara saw Maceo and his funk band play live in New York City, she claims, it felt as much like dance as it did music. All the band members riffed off each other, and it felt as natural as a conversation. They were all onstage together, working as a unit.

Explaining the Bandleader Archetype

What It Is

- You act as a role model for your team and lead by example.

- You actively participate in the group while also offering support and guidance.

- You provide support for individuals when they ask, yet your focus is on creating a positive group vibe.

- You are respected because of your vision, expertise, and leadership qualities.

When It Works

- Your team is high functioning and highly competent.

- You want your team to cocreate with you.

What You Gain

- A high degree of trust.

- Collaboration and creativity from all team members.

- Ability to be informal in your communication and relationship building.

What You Trade

- Prescriptive control—it may be harder to delegate or directly provide instruction.

- Formal boundaries—you will need to know when and where to draw a boundary and set clear expectations on behavioral norms within the team.

Remote Best Practices

- Be in the virtual trenches with your team. If you have asynchronous stand-ups on Slack or your project management tool, share what you are working on and your struggles.

- Celebrate wins. Highlight and encourage behaviors you see happening in your digital space. A quick emoji can go a long way.

- Don't always be the leader. Rotate roles, especially in meetings, to give others a chance to lead.

How to Flex

- Being a Bandleader increases your team's autonomy and will likely increase their work satisfaction. It will also give you a chance to sink your teeth into some content or code, which can be a refreshing change of pace.

- Try acting as a Bandleader in low-complexity situations. When can you allow other team members to rise to the challenge of leadership? What situations exist today that can be opportunities to practice flexing this style?

The Bandleader: In Real Life (IRL)

When we asked Anne McCarthy of Automattic about her management style, she referred to herself as a "walk alongside you" leader. She's heavily involved in the team's day-to-day work and often does the same things she's asking her team to do. She gives her team ownership and autonomy over their workflow. Her presence enables her to adapt to and evolve the team's changing needs; her deep expertise gives her a lens for coaching and skill development.

Phil Freo, VP product and engineering at Close.com, generally tries to be a hands-off manager, though he often errs on the side of Promoter (our next style coming up) over Bandleader. When he flexes to Bandleader, it is usually to build understanding. "I try to push some code, even if it's something extremely tiny. Every single time, I learn something, like 'Ah, there's so much pain in our developer environment.' It gives me more empathy."

The Promoter: Brian Epstein, "The Fifth Beatle"

Lady luck struck Brian Epstein on November 9, 1961. That fateful day at the Cavern Club in Liverpool, Brian first heard the Beatles perform at a lunchtime concert; the rest is history. Less than three months later, Brian became the Beatles' manager—eventually garnering him a unique role in the band as the legendary "Fifth Beatle."

Brian knew his place. The Beatles had talent, magic, and mojo; he didn't need to interfere. Instead, he did what he did best: managing all the moving pieces with third parties outside of the band—contracts, gigs, promotions—so he could set the Beatles up for success.

Like Brian Epstein, when you're a Promoter, you are your team's biggest fan, and you want to make big things happen for them. You're championing them for promotions, you're knocking down the doors of the marketing team for a bigger budget, and you're fighting for the resources they need to be successful. Given your outward orientation, your day is likely filled with meetings with other teams, but you make sure you're available to give guidance and help your team shine.

Explaining the Promoter Archetype

What It Is

- You act as the organization-facing leader for your team, ensuring that they have the right tools and resources to do their job and championing their success within the company.

- You support your team yet assume they will proactively come to you with challenges or requests for help.

- You expect your team to reach results based on their abilities and direction.

- Your team respects you because of your ability to help influence the rest of the company.

When It Works

- Your team is high functioning and highly competent.

- Relationships and stakeholders outside your core team are important to cultivate.

What You Gain

- Organizational influence—your team will have connections and resources within the broader organization.

- Information and insight—you will also have critical knowledge to take back to your team about the company's activities and broader goals.

What You Trade

- Direct team control—you may not be the person making day-to-day decisions.

- Regular involvement and collaboration with the team.

Remote Best Practices

- Manage information flow. Have a dedicated online space, such as Slack or Discord, to share your learnings. Ask your team to highlight things they want to be shared.

- Extend meeting invites. Don't feel the need to promote alone! Do you have a star employee and a meeting request at a time zone better suited for them? Let them take it. Seek opportunities to get your team directly involved in the larger organization. Building these connections will be mutually beneficial.

How to Flex

- You'll want to flex to the Promoter style at critical moments in your team's evolution. For example, annual planning, budget discussions, and hiring decisions tend to be when you'll need to represent your team within the broader organization.

- If your team is more senior, this style can also be great to ensure that they have visibility into organizational-wide decisions. As a Promoter, you act as the conduit of knowledge.

- This can be an excellent position to take if there is unequal influence or respect within the company (e.g., you manage a team of designers in a developer-focused company culture).

The Promoter in Real Life (IRL)

Steph Yiu, the chief customer officer of WordPress VIP, sees her role as helping her employees "do the best work they've done in their career." She knows how to pull specific levers to get employees the opportunities and resources.

Steph often finds herself in a position to recommend people for promotions or strategize on career growth. When employees ask her for their next challenge, it is up to her to say, "Yep, I can help you try a management role or try a senior IC role." Or "Nope, I can't give that to you now. Can we work on it together, or can we try again in six months?"

Steph thrives as a manager when her employees know what they want. It's clear how to move forward and make things happen within the broader organization.

The Agent: SM Entertainment, K-Pop

The Agent describes a manager who is tactically involved in the team's day-to-day activities. The flow of information tends to be top-down, and as a manager, you have particular expectations, roles, and methods of approaching work for your team.

For example, SM Entertainment's role in the notorious K-pop girl band, Girls' Generation. It is not easy to be part of this group. It requires up to five years of training before debuting for the first time onstage. But it's worth it. Girls' Generation was the first girl group to have four music videos with over 100 million views *each* on You-Tube. That's more than 3,044 years of collective watch time. (Think about that for a second.)

Their lives, though, are tightly controlled. Their songs are written by their agent, SM Entertainment, which also lines up endorsement deals. There's a formula for success, and SM Entertainment knows it, inside and out. They control the entire process, from scouting to training to performing.

When you're managing like an Agent, you control every detail of your team's work and are also very concerned about external perception. This may be important if you're a civil engineering manager and any mistake could result in public harm, but in general, it is this archetype that we caution you to use with care.

Explaining the Agent Archetype

What It Is

- You generally take a more autocratic approach to delegate work to your team.

- You provide individual support for team members through highly directive processes, instructions, and expectation setting.

- You are respected because of your formal role.

When It Works

- Your team has talent but requires training and apprenticeship.

- You need to control the external and internal elements to be successful.

What You Gain

- Team control—you can assign tasks and responsibilities without much forward planning.

- Output control—you have a high degree of oversight and provide multiple rounds of feedback before completing a final project.

What You Trade

- Input and creative contributions from team members.

- Self-motivation of employees that stems from autonomy and self-direction.

- Sense of trust and flexibility on the team.

Remote Best Practices

- Create a container. When you break projects down into specific tasks, you can act as an Agent within particular tasks, such as singular meetings, without risking team autonomy.

- We recommend using this type of management style in limited capacities due to the risk of hindering motivation, decreasing productivity, and discouraging one of the most significant benefits of remote work: freedom.

How to Flex

- You'll want to flex to the Agent style when setting up the scaffolding of your team. It's vital to lay the proper foundation within the team—hiring the right people, training them, outlining their work—and foster the right external relationships to be successful.

The Agent in Real Life (IRL)

There's a time and a place for this management style, but use it carefully! Siobhan McKeown, the COO of Human Made, believes that "[m]icromanagement does not work in remote work. You cannot micromanage unless someone is really struggling. If someone is burned out, I'll go through their to-do list with them and help them prioritize. I'll help them look at their work in different ways."

Akshay Kapur, head of coaching at Automattic, commented on a few situations requiring a more directive style: "If you have a project deadline coming up, then as a leader, you may need to be more direct and speed-oriented. There might be quick updates around what's necessary, which might be very directive. It might even be uncomfortable for a leader who's more of a servant leader."

The Composer: Ludwig van Beethoven

Some managers, like the Composers, can see (or hear) the bigger piece of the puzzle and work to place the pieces accordingly. Managers with this style may expect different things from each employee based on their unique strengths and work with them to delegate roles as they see fit, expecting employees to follow a process, but are not necessarily interested in details of lesser importance.

Take Beethoven, for example. At 21, he left his dysfunctional home to study under Joseph Haydn. Nearly a decade later, he performed his first symphony, appropriately named Symphony No. 1, at the K. K. Hoftheater nächst der Burg in Vienna. Flutes, oboes, clarinets, bassoons, horns, trumpets, timpani, violins, violas, cellos, and contrabasses played for 25 minutes. Beethoven had a vision and a plan. The musicians needed to play the musical notes precisely as he'd written. This left little room for autonomy or self-direction but resulted in a work of beauty.

The Composer tends to have a rigid process. If a flute player goes off script, it can ruin the song for everyone. However, the Composer is deeply involved in the team's work and is receptive to feedback. They love to hear ideas and suggestions from the flute player on how to change the process (or, in this case, the composition)—just not in the middle of a performance.

You might need to flex into the Composer role when in the execution phase. Perhaps you're a product manager, and your team needs to launch a new feature built to spec by a specific date. There's no time to debate or rehash previous decisions. Or maybe you're a marketer, and your team is creating a commercial. There's no time to go back on creative decisions once shooting.

Explaining the Composer Archetype

What It Is

- You are an expert at seeing the big picture and how everyone can play a role.

- You create and provide specific processes, instructions, and expectations for your team and then expect them to execute independently.

- You delegate work based on your team members' unique skill sets and interests.

- You are respected because of how you take individual work preferences into account.

When It Works

- Your work requires the ability to follow processes, but you believe in your team's abilities to get it done autonomously.

- There is a transparent process or directions to follow, and you are open to feedback on the process itself.

- You are skilled at guiding your team on complex tasks.

What You Gain

- Ensuring task completion on a regular cadence.

- A balance of autonomy and directive control.

- Removes guesswork—you know the process that will be followed and can quickly check in on work as desired.

What You Trade

- Creativity from discovering new ways of doing things.

- Potential demotivator if the process is too limiting. There should still be room for autonomy and flexibility for team members.

Remote Best Practices

- Embrace documentation. To balance autonomy and direction, you must use the process, not yourself and your personality, to manage.

- Reinforce behaviors over tools. Provide feedback on the behaviors you observe within the tools rather than the tools themselves. Are they setting expectations in your project management system? Are they documenting their code in GitHub? Focus on expectation setting, clear communication, and streamlining tasks, and less on how often team members log in.

How to Flex

- You'll want to flex to the Composer style when execution is paramount. The buy-in is there; now it's time to get things done. To flex to this style, develop a work plan and have clear checkpoints for accountability.

- Documentation skills become paramount. Learn how to record the structure, workflow, and knowledge base so that your team can learn, understand, and find answers to their questions independently. You maintain control but are not a roadblock to getting things done.

The Composer in Real Life (IRL)

Zbigniew Motak described his former manager and our coauthor Ali at DuckDuckGo as a Composer: "You empower through delegation. If it's not formal delegation, you see what they're interested in and make sure they can work on it."

Ali spent most of her time creating and building new processes from scratch instead of directing her team on what to do and when. When her teammates were tasked with leading projects, they could follow the processes and iterate on them. That was how Zbigniew came to perfect the project stage of the interview process for candidates, while another employee, Bill, managed first-round interviews and early-stage communication with candidates.

❓ REFLECTION QUESTIONS

1. Which management style most defines you naturally?
2. How is your style valuable to your team? How can it be challenging?
3. Given your role and your team, which management style makes the most sense?
4. How might you flex to adapt to that management style?

BUILDING CONSCIOUS LEADERSHIP

You have learned more about yourself and your working preferences from the Mad Libs exercise. You can see how to flex between management styles based on the situation according to the RW Manager Archetypes.

To put it into practice, you'll need to hone your self-awareness skills further. You need to be able to read the team's ever-changing landscape to decide what style is required. You'll need to reflect upon your actions and communication style to understand how they impact your team.

That's no easy feat! So we looked to a few current and former executive coaches for advice on becoming a conscious leader.

Attunement

When Tam asked Akshay Kapur, head of coaching at Automattic, what coaching skill could immediately apply to managers, his answer was clear: attunement. Akshay explained:

It's the ability to meet the other person where they're at in the moment. And that includes meeting oneself where they're at that moment. . . . Your ability to pay attention to what's in between you and the other person is my definition of attunement.

An example is how you and I had scheduled a call last time, and I felt like I had a headache. I was out of it and didn't feel like I would be able to show up. I communicated that with you, and you were kind enough to reschedule.

Or let's say you came onto the call, and you said, "I feel like I'm pushing through here; maybe this is not the right time to talk." That's a simple example of meeting someone where they're *not*.

A complex example is when somebody says, "I don't think I'm good at delegation." And at that moment, you can give advice. You can share your experience. You can talk to somebody about why they think that. You can ask them to provide an example. There are so many ways to go.

Attunement can look like an unscripted dance (a client's actual term to describe one of Akshay's coaching sessions). Rather than coming in with a plan or methodology, he chooses to go into the room "empty." Through this practice, Akshay can be attentive to the other person's needs at the moment—both verbal and nonverbal—to understand where and how they're struggling.

Akshay might offer tactical advice or tell a personal story based on those cues. He might ask a question or take a breath and pause. Not everything needs to be fixed; sometimes, people need space and the confidence to fix it themselves. Consider this advice:

A remarkable outcome of being open is that people become vulnerable, sensitive, and even emotional at times. When there is nothing wanted of them, and you hold a genuine belief that they are OK as they are, it can be unnerving to those for whom high expectations are a norm. Their nervous system is no longer on alert, and it can relax. And when it does, sometimes personal or professional emotions pour out. The coaching space is not meant to be therapeutic, but holding a stance of complete openness can be therapeutic in and of itself. I'm quite moved when this happens.

Building Trust

Taylor Jacobson, CEO of Focusmate and a former executive coach, emphasized the need for managers to build their "trust muscles." It might not come naturally, especially when there is a lot at stake, like your reputation, a deadline, or an expectation by your boss. "It's about being willing not to push someone to get something done but trusting that people are intrinsically motivated. And frankly, pushing them to value their well-being higher. Many on our team have experienced burnout and have experienced major health issues due to overwork and overstress. We're creating a workplace where we actively talk about those things."

Darcy Boles echoed a similar sentiment about building your trust muscles as a remote worker. "I think it takes six months to two years to fully trust yourself to work remotely, like truly remote. Getting on a phone with somebody instead of a video call takes a certain amount of trust."

Darcy still remembers a new employee who asked if they could go to the bathroom, and she was baffled until she thought more about it. "The place they had come from was very regimented—industrial revolution style. They were clocking in and clocking out, and they had to be at their desks all of the time. This person was now remote and didn't know what to do with their freedom. They didn't trust themselves or me yet to design their life around their work."

If you've been told that work looks one way, and suddenly the paradigm shifts, it can be scary and disorienting, like when an animal is finally let out of its cage but is too afraid to explore.

Darcy suggests that remote workers challenge each other to do something scary in the middle of the day—even if it's simply a midday walk at first. If not, you'll keep seeing fallback into familiar nine-to-five patterns. Instead, Darcy encourages her team "to manage their energy instead of their time."

Walking the Talk

Ben Brooks, a former executive coach and the CEO of PILOT, an employee development platform, highlighted the need for managers to walk the talk. If you're expecting certain norms and behaviors from your team, you need to model them as a manager.

For example, Ben encourages his team to establish work-life boundaries. He wants them to be able to unplug at the end of the day. That being said, Ben also has a personal preference as a business owner to answer emails after hours when it's quieter, and his calendar is free.

To balance the needs of his team (work-life boundaries) and his needs (to answer emails after hours), he compromises. He knows that sending a rush of emails at 10 p.m. will overwhelm his team (it's hard to say no to CEO emails at night), so instead he schedules the emails to go out the following day at 8 a.m. It's a small gesture that goes a long way.

❓ REFLECTION QUESTIONS

1. How can you pay attention to what's between you and your employees? When should you step in and give directive advice, versus when should you step back and listen?

2. How can you challenge your team to take advantage of the flexibility and freedom of remote work life?

3. Do your actions match your words? If not, what's a change you can make this week?

Managers and their teams are the heartbeat of an organization. If they stop functioning, the organization dies. Your influence as a manager will impact your team members and the direction of your organization.

Remember: Know thyself. Flex your style. And stay conscious of the adapting needs of your team. It's a big responsibility, but the power already lies inside you. We believe in you!

◉ ALI'S ADVICE

Before you dig into what tools to use, how to look better on video chat, or which virtual team-building activities aren't too lame, you need to build a strong foundation internally. The most significant shift you will need to make as a remote leader is self-awareness. Everything stems from self-awareness.

The more you figure out who you are as a leader, what you enjoy about managing, what your quirks are, and how it translates to a remote environment, the easier it will be to set expectations and build trust.

☺ TAM'S TIPS

If you're wired toward idealism or altruism, it can be helpful to see your role as a manager as more of a vocation than a job. Your actions will impact the emotional well-being of those on your team or project. Find ways to make it a worthwhile experience, and you'll be making a positive impact in the world every day.

CHAPTER THREE

Managing Your Remote Employee

🎯 TL;DR

This chapter focuses on how you engage with your remote employees, whether that's short-term collaboration on a project or taking an advisory role to help someone grow in their career. It is all about having a direct one-to-one impact.

At the end of this chapter, you'll be able to do the following:

✓ Bust common remote work myths to succeed where other managers have failed.

✓ Stop the hand-holding and micromanagement. Transform your employees' motivation and confidence by meeting their needs for security, autonomy, mastery, and connection.

✓ Develop great working relationships with your employees through tools like the RW Collaboration Kickoff and RW User Guide because isn't it best when everyone understands one another?

LOOKING BACK, Ali can see that one of her biggest challenges as a remote manager was learning to let go. Sound familiar?

She has always held high expectations for herself. In her days at McGill University, she was notorious for creating study books, flash cards, and practice exams, which she carried around with her at all times leading up to finals, from the dining hall to the gym and, yes, even the pub. Not surprisingly, when she entered the corporate world, those same expectations fell onto the people she managed. She was unafraid to push her employees out of their comfort zones and routinely demanded high-quality outputs.

Ali remembers one particular employee whom she managed at DuckDuckGo, Bill, who challenged her approach. Bill joined Duck-DuckGo in the company's early days as a jack-of-all-trades, well before Ali. She was asked to manage Bill when she joined full-time, which made her cautious. She wondered why he was interested in People Ops and if he'd have the right skill set to lead complicated people projects.

And so, to recount this story in full transparency for this book, Ali called Bill to reflect. "There were about 30 people in the company," said Bill, "and we started to think about People Ops, even though other companies didn't do that until much later. I felt like it was probably daunting for you to get a new employee, but for me, this is what I wanted to contribute to the company and to my growth."

Even though Bill was a junior-level employee at the company, he was eager to learn. As his manager, Ali decided on a great first task for Bill to own: implementing the new calendaring system across the company. This was intentional. Ali thought it would utilize his get-things-done attitude and his knowledge of the inner workings (and complaints) across the organization. Sure, the task sounds banal. But if you've ever tried scheduling meetings across multiple time zones, you know how important this is, especially in a remote, global organization!

To help Bill out, Ali structured the problem for him. After all, it was Bill's first time owning a complex project instead of completing individual tasks. She laid out the problem to be solved, discussed milestones, and reviewed the communication plan—and then she waited. She wanted to balance supporting Bill with seeing what Bill could accomplish on his own.

Bill recalls this experience as putting his feet in the fire. "It was good, but I couldn't believe I would be responsible for shaping how the company would collaborate."

After a few days, Ali checked their project management tool, only to be disappointed. While technically on time, Bill's analysis of potential calendaring systems did not include his rationale leading up to his final recommendation. Plus, the final result was not structured as she would have done it. (Can you imagine?) She had pictured a beautifully organized, color-coded spreadsheet; instead, she got a bulleted checklist of requirements. How had Bill not read her mind! She regretted not checking in with Bill earlier to influence the outcome.

On their call, Bill shared more about why he had taken that approach years earlier:

> My previous career adviser would have told me, "Why are you wasting so much time putting this in that format? Just write it down. Get it out there." And then you were like, "What is this? Why isn't this formatted?" I was just dumping ideas for the different approaches into different headers in Asana with the [pros and cons] underneath them.

Ali realized, first, and foremost, that not everyone works like her. Second, she would not have the patience or bandwidth to continually check up on Bill's project management methods and his color-coding expertise (as exciting as that may sound). Frankly, Ali realized that those details did not matter. She was acting like an Agent but wanted to be a Composer.

That experience made Ali recognize that she wanted to be a different type of manager: one that would set the vision for her team and then collaborate, rather than dictating how the work should be done. She wanted to inspire Bill and help him develop as a People Ops leader. Over time, she learned how to do this.

Bill grew in his career and was promoted several times. He's proud of how far he's come. According to Bill, "It was still early in my career. I was learning how to manage expectations asynchronously and scope and run a project. Before that, I was just completing tasks. It was daunting at first, and it took a lot of coaching from you to help me feel comfortable. Now it's second nature. Now I think that this is easy and how you work. It's a muscle you have to flex."

Ali also grew from this experience as a manager using the exercises we'll explore in this chapter. Another former employee described her as "an empathetic leader, who draws a clear vision and rallies people behind it. Her coaching and mentoring skills are second to none."

Ali had learned her lesson! Are you ready to learn some of your own?

Take a moment and reflect on your managers:

> *Which ones did you learn from?*

> *Which ones did you trust?*

For example, Tam learned everything she knows about pricing analysis and complicated stakeholder management from one of her favorite managers, whom her team nicknamed GGG ("Good guy, Gabe"). She trusted him because he was smart, diligent, caring, and committed.

On the other hand, we're sure you've had managers of whom just the thought brings back bad memories. Maybe they made you feel small or were manipulative. Or no matter how much you tried, your work was never right in their eyes.

As the saying goes, people leave managers, not companies. Managers can make or break an employee's work experience—which means that as a manager, you have a critical role to play.

Darcy Boles believes most people move to all-remote companies seeking a different work experience. "They've been brought to their knees in the past," she said, explaining that great remote management is an opportunity to show up for people in a way opposite from the negative way they were treated in the past.

This chapter is all about helping employees overcome challenges and preparing them to contribute to the team. No matter what type of manager you are or what archetype comes naturally to you, there's an opportunity to build trust further and inspire your employees.

In this chapter, we'll dispel common myths about remote workers, stand on the shoulders of giants, and learn how motivation theory can apply to remote management. We'll wrap up with a practical RW Collaboration Kickoff agenda and RW User Guide to help you start your working relationship off on the right foot with your employees. Let's go!

DISPELLING COMMON MYTHS

You might have some hesitations at this point. Sure, it sounds great ... in writing. Of course, you'd like to be the "best manager" you can be, but there is a lot stacked up against *remote* managers. Haven't you been reading the news?

Fair. Let's start by exploring the challenges you've experienced or read about remote management.

Check the statements you believe to be true that follow.

- ☐ It's hard to know when remote employees are being productive.

- ☐ Remote work leads to mental health challenges like isolation or loneliness.

- ☐ There's no accountability.

- ☐ I can't trust my remote workers.

- ☐ Remote workers procrastinate and fly under the radar more.

- ☐ All remote employees feel isolated.

- ☐ Remote workers are only productive because they work too much! I'm worried about burnout.

- ☐ You'll never really know your coworkers.

Tally up your checkmarks.

0–3: You generally feel comfortable managing remotely.

4–6: You're undecided. Some aspects of working remotely work, but it could be better.

7–8: You have your doubts (understandably!). We'll do our best to myth-bust.

Regardless of where you are on the scale, we're excited to empower you with techniques to bust these common remote work myths on your watch!

While these myths make great (and by that we mean clickable) headlines on social media, they are not always true. Some remote workers struggle with productivity and isolation, while others find it motivating when there's an enticing reward nearby, like a nap or watching a movie.

There's a kernel of truth to all these remote work myths. We believe they are primarily caused by employees not having the correct information, tools, or coaching to work effectively remotely. And guess what, that's *your* job as a manager.

STANDING ON THE SHOULDERS OF GIANTS: MOTIVATION THEORY

As we examined these myths and their root causes, we kept coming back to motivation theory. *What drives someone at work? Is it different in a remote context?*

To answer those two questions, we scoured the various frameworks with a remote state of mind, such as Daniel Pink's *Drive*, Self-Determination Theory, Maslow's Hierarchy of Needs, the SCARF model, Herzberg's Motivators and Hygiene Factors, and even the Big 5 Personality Traits, and we found that they all laddered up to similar themes. For employees to stay motivated, their needs for security, autonomy, mastery, and connection must be met.

1. **Security:** Employees believe that the organization will fulfill its promises and that they can bring their full self to work without punishment.

2. **Autonomy:** Employees can determine how, where, and when they work.

3. **Mastery:** Employees can showcase their expertise and grow skills.

4. **Connection:** Employees understand how they fit into the team and organization.

Ideas in Practice: Managing Your Employees' Need for Security

Employees need to feel safe and secure at work before they can perform. For example, employees need to feel fairly compensated. If working in an office, they need a clean space in which to work without risk of injury.

In remote work, security might look different. For example, an employee needs to access the same information as everyone else on the team, which sounds obvious. But how often is essential information exchanged in hallway conversations, especially in hybrid organizations? If you use videoconferencing, you might need to feel comfortable showing your home office space, even if it looks different from your colleagues'.

Manager Mantra

I will help my employees get their basic work needs met. (Some I can directly control, and others I can influence.)

Types of Security Needs

As a remote manager, you can help employees feel secure at work through the following:

- **Policies and rules:** You help employees understand what is acceptable at work.

- **Tools:** You make sure that employees have the resources to do their work.

- **Role expectations:** You set and reset expectations of the role.

- **Psychological safety:** You create an environment where all employees feel comfortable speaking up without the risk of punishment or humiliation.

- **Fairness:** You take steps to make employees feel included and free from discrimination. You promote transparency, so that employees understand why and how specific projects are assigned.

- **Certainty:** You discuss the future of projects, the team, and the broader organization and help employees connect to their work.

Warning Signs

- If your team *does not* speak up when you ask for constructive feedback, they may be worried about retaliation.

- If employees *rarely* join Zoom calls with their cameras on, they might not be comfortable inviting work into their personal spaces.

⌕ SPOTLIGHT STORY: Diversity and Inclusion in a Remote Context

Outside of Anne McCarthy's day job as a developer relations wrangler at Automattic (yes, that's an actual title), she is a force of nature around all topics DEI (diversity, equity, and inclusion) both at work and on her blog.

When we asked Anne to define DE&I, she leaned on a Vernā Myers quote: "Diversity is being invited to the party; inclusion is being asked to dance."

As Anne aptly put it, "We spend a large majority of our lives working. It's damaging to compartmentalize major parts of ourselves and exist in a bubble of sameness, dealing with constant microaggressions. How work is done matters just as much as what is accomplished. That's why organizations need to embrace these ideas deeply."

Anne recommends some habits for managers to lead a more inclusive team:

- Don't make assumptions about what your employee values around job satisfaction, career, etc. Lead with questions and same-paging exercises.

- Offer multiple ways for someone to give feedback on a decision, such as written, verbal, synchronous, and asynchronous, to accommodate the various ways that people process information. Ensure that there are multiple moments when feedback is collected (immediately or in a week).

- Provide extra context for your decisions, and be open to pushback from your team.

- Delay decision-making to be inclusive of those in different time zones.

- Don't always choose the first volunteer for a project. Make opportunities available to those who might be in a different time zone or more reserved.

- Remove slang from your language, especially when setting goals, to help with language barriers.

> **❓ REFLECTION QUESTIONS**
>
> 1. How do you already create a safe and inclusive environment for your team?
>
> 2. What's one way you can help your employees feel more secure at work?

Ideas in Practice: Managing Your Employees' Need for Autonomy

Nearly every remote expert we interviewed touched on the need for personal autonomy to make remote work *actually* work, which mirrored our own experience.

Autonomy can be a confusing term, though. The dictionary defines it as "the right or condition of self-government." But what does that look like in practice? Let's unpack autonomy together and explore how it looks in a remote context.

Manager Mantra

I will help my employees design a work environment that suits their skills, working styles, and personal preferences.

Types of Autonomy Needs

Remote work permits more autonomy than a traditional office. Employees can decide how the job gets done and where (and often when). For you as a manager, it is important to recognize different modes of autonomy so that you can help your employees successfully adjust to this new way of working.

- **Environment:** The need to adjust surroundings for novelty or routine. If possible, give your team time (and budget) to set up an ideal working environment or find a coworking space outside the home.

- **Schedule:** The need to organize work around personal life and biorhythms. Work asynchronously when possible so that team members can craft their work schedules.

- **Control:** The need to feel in control of job inputs and outputs. Give employees the support and information they need to complete their work independently.

- **Learning style:** The need to process information in a particular format. Incorporate different forms of communication—written, video, and audio.

- **Socialization:** The need for solo time or team time. Suggest optional social events, and give your team the freedom to organize hangouts together on their own. For example, at Hotjar, they have Gamejar, a group for active gamers, and a Strava group, where fitness fanatics can log their miles together.

Warning Signs

- Employees feel a need to overcommunicate when they will be away from their computer or working from a different location than usual—for example, sharing when they are taking lunch breaks or have midday appointments, even when it is not a team norm.

- Employees frequently check in for feedback on the work itself and ask permission before moving on to the next project stage. Employees may not feel a sense of autonomy if they rely too much on input for minor steps in the project.

When Cody Jones of Zapier transitioned from in-person to remote management, he found that leading with a vision helped his team embrace their autonomy:

You have to lead with a strong vision, but it can't just be that. You also have to document it. People need to see it, know it, and be able to recite it back. Second, you need to give them clear goals. People want to be autonomous, but they're not going to be successful unless they have clear goals. Then, you can let people define their productivity. It's not the hours in the day. It's not whether they're in the office or not. It's hitting those goals and being excited about it.

We agree with Cody's advice. One additional tip: it can be helpful to have your team help set the vision. That way, they're more invested from the get-go.

> **❓ REFLECTION QUESTIONS**
>
> 1. What's one way that you can help your employees feel more autonomous?
> 2. What would change if you trusted your employees from day one?

Ideas in Practice: Fostering Your Employees' Need for Mastery

It feels *good* to do *good work*. Just ask Jaclyn Rice Nelson and Noah Gale, the cofounders of Tribe AI, a new take on the freelancing/consulting model for machine learning and artificial intelligence (ML/AI) engineers.

When asked about the value proposition for engineers in their collective, they immediately referenced personal freedom and exciting work. "Work that they're extremely well-suited for and are set up for success. [They want to] not just do interesting work, but do it well. No one wants to do work they're not going to do well."

Darcy Boles takes it a step further through role shaping and role casting. "I look at formulating remote teams based on people's strengths instead of expecting that people will be good at everything."

Let's see how you can set your employees up to do *good work*!

Manager Mantra

I will help my employees succeed in their roles.

Types of Mastery Needs

While most, if not all, employees desire to reach mastery in their functional expertise, the *how* and *why* might vary. Recognizing the underlying motivation will help you offer recognition or rewards appropriately. Here are a few underlying mastery motivations:

- **Ownership:** The need for decision-making. Find ways for employees to become key stakeholders in projects.

- **Efficacy:** The need to see results. Ask employees to be part of the testing phase of the work itself.

- **Status:** The need to be recognized. Say thank you and give recognition when an employee has gone above and beyond in their work.

- **Growth:** The need to see personal progress. Provide constructive feedback and stretch goals.

Warning Signs

- Projects do not have clear owners or stakeholders, and there's no central place to see who is leading specific projects. Employees are hesitant to provide updates on the projects they own.

- There are no virtual signs of a "thank you" culture. When you log in to communication and project management tools, you do not see congratulatory remarks when people have accomplished their goals.

- Your employees are hesitant to take on stretch goals and do not ask for feedback.

🔍 SPOTLIGHT STORY: Respecting Your Employees' Expertise

Taylor Jacobson, CEO of Focusmate, trusts his team's expertise, so much so that he encourages them to make the decisions. "I am exceedingly cautious about imposing a decision on anyone unless I feel strongly about it."

He asks his team to come to him with recommendations, not vice versa. "I think it starts with them bringing the recommendation, talking about it, and expanding the scope of what they can decide without your input over time. . . . Our team has found it exhilarating and highly unusual to feel trusted so much. They know the buck isn't getting passed. The decision is on them."

We believe that Taylor's method meets employees' need for mastery and creates a coaching moment. As employees become more decisive, they'll be able to work more autonomously.

> ### ❓ REFLECTION QUESTIONS
>
> 1. How can you shape roles to play to your employees' strengths?
> 2. How can you build your employees' decision-making capability?

Ideas in Practice: Managing Your Employees' Need for Connection

Never in our lives have we heard so many people commiserate about the loss of water-cooler conversations. What was once a punch line in shows like *The Office* has become an artifact of nostalgia.

To fill that space, we've seen managers (in good faith) schedule remote happy hours and more check-in meetings to make sure that remote employees feel connected. But what if connection isn't about meetings and water coolers after all?

We often assume that connections are interpersonal, but in remote, connection to the company's mission and values plays an even greater role, giving employees a sense of purpose in their work. In remote, you cannot rely on the bells and whistles of a fancy office to mask unsatisfying work.

For example, Hotjar sees its core values as its "secret sauce" for employee engagement. According to Ken Weary, "They're more than just words on a wall. They're used weekly to make strategic business decisions and tactical on-the-ground ones." Leadership at Hotjar even stack-ranked the five values, so they know which one wins out if two are in contention. By putting their values into action, Hotjar creates a deep sense of connection between employees and their work.

Manager Mantra

I will help my employees feel connected to their work and their role within the team.

Types of Connection Needs

It's natural to assume that "connection" means more communication, but in remote, connecting to an organization's mission or enjoying the work itself often matters just as much, if not more. Here are a few modes of connection:

- **Purpose:** Employees feel connected to work. Help employees find meaning by connecting the dots between their day-to-day activities and higher-level goals and mission.

- **Position:** Employees need to understand why they exist in the team and organization. Help them by highlighting the unique skill set they bring to the team.

- **Belonging:** Employees need to feel seen and heard. Make a social space for employees to connect about work and personal interests.

Warning Signs

- Lack of personal chatter on employee-based Slack channels and during team meetings. It might signal unaddressed conflict.

- Employees question the importance of their projects. They might not understand why their work matters (sometimes, rightfully so!).

- Employees lack engagement with you during regular one-on-one meetings. They may lack trust or feel burned out.

🔍 SPOTLIGHT STORY: Spotting Employee Disengagement and Burnout Remotely

You're not going to have the same nonverbal cues you might have observed in an office. You won't be able to easily see if employees are staying late or seem on edge. Instead, you'll need to find ways to accomplish that remotely.

Chase Warrington, the head of remote at Doist, believes the role of an everyday manager is "to keep employees from burning out" and to "keep tabs on how their life is going personally and how that connects to their professional life."

He spends 75 percent of his time asking his team questions like these: How are you doing? How's the workload? How can I support you? And it's not just asking the questions but creating a space where the employee can answer honestly. They are not real questions unless the employee is free to respond with "I need help, ASAP" or "This workload is way too much for one person" without punishment.

Cody Jones of Zapier initially found it challenging to adapt his in-person management skills to remote. "I thought I was a good leader at my last company. People are my strong suit. That's why I'm in partnerships. It felt like I was fighting with my arms tied behind my back or without oxygen when I moved to remote leadership. It was like my superpowers were gone. Leadership in the remote world is an absolute talent that needs investment."

Cody eventually found his remote leadership groove. For example, he's mastered the art of reading emotion from simple interactions. Even small details like a missing emoji or exclamation point might signal to Cody that he needs to check in with the person.

He is also intentional about creating a safety net for his team. "You can get in your head when you don't see and interact with people. Others don't know that you're down, and if you fail, you can beat yourself up mentally." Cody encourages his team to be open about failures, learn from them, and try something different.

Darcy Boles sees her role similarly: "I'm a highly sensitive person. People have called me a barometer. There are a lot of remote managers who feel like we have a spidey sense." Darcy proactively reads through the social channels at least once a week to find the last "big conversation." She checks for variance in tone of voice, emoji use, and comment frequency. If it's more or less than usual, she'll ask a few questions to see what is happening.

Of course, you need to adjust your method to the norms of your organization. We encourage you to find your way to connect with your employees and spot potential issues and burnout. These are the key things to remember: Are you connecting on a personal level to your employees and creating a safe space where they can share openly? Do you have enough awareness of communication norms at work that you can spot unusual behavior or red flags? If the answer to either of those questions is no, ask yourself how you can continue to build a connection and trust between you.

❓ REFLECTION QUESTIONS

1. How can you help your employees see how they contribute to the team and organization?

2. What is one thing you can do to create stronger connections for your employees?

THE MANAGER'S ROLE: ENABLING YOUR EMPLOYEES' SUCCESS

We've covered a lot, so let's go back to the basics. Your role as a manager is to meet your employees' tactical and emotional needs so that they can succeed in their roles. You can use the pillars of human motivation (security, autonomy, mastery, and connection) to troubleshoot problems (table 3.1).

Remember, you're building your remote manager muscles. It's OK to struggle. It's OK not to get it right the first time. It's OK to feel uncomfortable at times.

Even remote work experts feel growing pains along the way. For example, Taylor Jacobson told us, "I remember going through this transition. I felt that if I shared that I played tennis during the day today, my team would start messing around. It's going to be game

TABLE 3.1 Recapping the Pillars of Motivation

THE NEED	THE MANTRA	THE MANIFESTATIONS
Security	I will help my employees get their basic work needs met.	• Policies and rules • Tools • Role expectations • Psychological safety • Fairness • Certainty
Autonomy	I will help my employees design a work environment that suits their skills, working styles, and personal preferences.	• Environment • Schedule • Control • Learning style • Socialization
Mastery	I will help my employees succeed in their roles.	• Ownership • Efficacy • Status • Growth
Connection	I will help my employees feel connected to their work and their role within the team.	• Purpose • Position • Belonging

over. Or if I shared that I've been stressed out and haven't been able to focus, it wouldn't be consistent with my image of 'I'm getting shit done all the time.' That it'd be a carte blanche to screw around."

Thankfully, Taylor can hardly remember the days when he struggled in this way, but he can still remember that underlying fear of being vulnerable with his team while sharing his ups and downs.

PUTTING IT INTO PRACTICE: RW COLLABORATION KICKOFF AND USER GUIDE

It takes vulnerability and, in some ways, a leap of faith to move from micromanaging to trusting in your team's intrinsic motivations. We want you to get from Point A to Point B as quickly as possible, so we've outlined two processes to help.

RW Collaboration Kickoff

You've likely heard of a project kickoff. Those rigorous plans and meetings with key stakeholders ensure that everyone is on the same page. They're important. They're necessary. But why do they exist only for projects, not for people?

At least, that was Ali's thought while a manager at DuckDuckGo.

- What would happen if people were as thoughtful about working together when kicking off a project for the first time?

- How can you codesign an excellent work experience with your employee?

- What if 20 minutes were spent up front discussing interpersonal dynamics instead of the project requirements?

There was only one way to answer her questions: to experiment! (In case you're wondering, the experiment was a success.) Eventually, the People Operations team built a people kickoff into the employee onboarding journey at DuckDuckGo. We've used her experience as inspiration for the RW Collaboration Kickoff, which can be used by a manager and employee or two peers working together.

🛠 HOW-TO: RW Collaboration Kickoff

The RW Collaboration Kickoff is a simple yet powerful exercise to start your working relationship with intentionality. It can be synchronous or asynchronous,[1] but the goals are the same: establish trust, learn about one another, understand the employee's motivations, and connect the dots to the broader organization.

Before getting started, it is essential to set the stage, explain the goal of the Collaboration Kickoff in your own words, and set intentions for your time together. You'll also want to discuss confidentiality and how the information discussed will be used. The following topics are agenda items we would recommend including in the meeting.

Introductions

Whether it's been a while since you worked together or the employee is new, you'll want to spend time learning about one another. We recommend that the manager go first and lead by example. You can share your focus at the company, more about your career trajectory, passions and obligations outside of work, and why you're working together.

Setting Role Expectations

This is a time to ask questions about the job to be done and get on the same page about the work. Questions may include the following:

- Do you and the employee have a shared understanding of the responsibilities required?

- What skill sets are needed to fulfill those responsibilities?

- What does the employee believe to be their strengths and gaps?

- What else would be useful to know about each other's skills and backgrounds?

Understanding Motivations

Once a baseline is developed, it is time to dig into the employee's working styles and needs for security, autonomy, mastery, and connection. You should repurpose and share the RW Working Style Preferences from chapter 2 with a few tweaks. You'll want to call out the similarities and differences and how they might impact your working together. Here are a few questions that may be appropriate:

- What are some must-haves when it comes to your working style and environment?

- How do you like to give and receive information and feedback?

- What do you want after this role? What's next, professionally?

- What makes you feel shiny at work?

• • • • • •

After the conversation, you will want to take time to connect the dots for your employee, as well as explain how the team and organization are structured, how the employee's role ladders up to the bigger picture of the team, and the purpose of the role. Finally, document the key learnings and agreements you made together in the RW User Guide. This will serve as an artifact from the RW Collaboration Kickoff and ensure that you're putting all the important things you learned about each other into practice! Plus, this will help you later when managing team dynamics, which we'll cover further in chapter 4.

✂ HOW-TO: RW User Guide

You will share and learn a lot during the RW Collaboration Kickoff. But, given that you're human, there is a chance you'll forget over time. Therefore, we recommend that you take a remote state of mind and document everything you learn (and more) in the RW User Guide.

You may be thinking, aren't user guides for objects? Yes, we agree. Now, imagine the last time you bought a kitchen gadget or some newfangled electronic device. It likely came with an instruction manual (with varying readability levels) to help you use the device and troubleshoot common problems.

While we highly recommend that you think of your employees as humans, not objects, we believe the same principles apply. Under what conditions do your employees work best? What makes them tick? What are their pet peeves? How can you manage them according to their needs?

Creating and relying on a personalized user guide is a best practice at many all-remote companies. We've used them at Oyster, DuckDuckGo, and Automattic.

Darcy Boles, for example, onboards new employees with an async questionnaire that asks: How do they like to be managed? How do they respond to feedback? What's their learning style? Taking an inventory of employee needs and styles up front helps her flex her style, especially with more introverted and neurodivergent team members.

Likewise, when Ali Brandt worked as a product manager at an international start-up, everyone created their own "user manual" in a one-page Google Doc that included topics like these: here's who I am, here's how I like to work, here's what I expect from the people I work with, here are my commitments, here's how I want you to communicate with me, here's my SLA ("service-level agreement") on how and when you can expect to hear back from me, here are my quirks, here are my pet peeves, and here's what makes me happy.

Ben Brooks incorporated a version of the user guide into his career development platform, PILOT. He encourages employees to write a guide on how they like to work, what's shaped their world-view, and what makes them unique/special/different.

Ben likens the User Guide to an API in the developer world. "[The User Guide] defines the interface with their colleagues. For instance, a late-night call may be a problem for one person and a preference for others." Ben believes that knowing this information is magic for working together. It's something that HR departments traditionally have a hard time figuring out.

User Guide: Do's and Don'ts

✓ Do make it a living document (things change!).

✓ Do make it actionable. Focus on information that impacts how you'll work together, like the following:
  ○ Work schedule and availability
  ○ Frequency, content, and medium of communication
  ○ How you like to give and receive feedback
  ○ Learning and communication styles
  ○ Quirks, pet peeves, and preferences

✓ Do make it easily digestible (one to two pages).

✗ Don't share with the broader team until you've received permission.
  ○ Some aspects of the RW Collaboration Kickoff are for the manager's eyes only (e.g., how the employee feels trusted and respected in the workplace, short-term and long-term professional goals, etc.).

• • • • • •

Let's switch gears. Remember the story about Ali, Bill, and the calendar tool from the beginning of this chapter?

Upon reflection, if Ali and Bill had scheduled an RW Collaboration Kickoff and documented their working preferences in an RW User Guide, many headaches could have been avoided. Here are a few lessons that Ali learned along the way.

- Ali values employees who show their work before a deadline. A quick update after completing major tasks helps her feel in the loop.

- Bill does not value showing his work. In his words, "It's like math problems. I hated when [an assignment] said show your work in school. Especially if I just knew the answer. I'm willing to do it, but it is not my go-to."

- Bill does not enjoy spending time "beautifying" work. He prefers taking a simple approach to sharing work when possible.

- It is helpful for both Ali and Bill to agree on expectations and deliverables up front.

- Bill wants to learn more about complex project management, one of Ali's strong suits. Ali could have focused her feedback for Bill on his organizational skills rather than the design aspects of the deliverable, helping Bill meet his need for mastery.

❓ REFLECTION QUESTIONS

1. When would an RW Collaboration Kickoff and RW User Guide have helped you start off a working relationship on better footing?

2. What information do you think should be included in an RW User Guide for your team?

♥ ALI'S ADVICE

Don't underestimate the power of the RW Collaboration Kick-off, even if you have been working with someone for years. I truly believe the root source of all conflict is mismatched expectations—so instead of assuming you know how best to work with someone, ask them how they like to work and set expectations together.

☺ TAM'S TIPS

Autonomy is key to remote work, though it's human to want to maintain control. Great remote managers know when to let go and when to let employees handle work independently. Think of it like learning to ride a bicycle. You may want to provide support at first (like training wheels), but eventually you should encourage your employees to ride on their own.

CHAPTER FOUR

Creating a Team Charter

🎯 TL;DR

We'll use Tuckman's Five Stages of Team Development—forming, storming, norming, performing, adjourning—as a map for this chapter, highlighting the telltale signs of each stage, looking at what's unique about remote, and outlining a few exercises you can test out with your team.

At the end of this chapter, you'll be able to do the following:

✓ Navigate each stage (from forming to adjourning) with ease, creating a high-functioning team.

✓ Successfully resolve tension on your team, as you go from storming to norming, ensuring unity and connection.

✓ Sit back, relax, and watch your team crush their goals once they hit the Performing stage.

✓ Give your team a proper farewell to be able to move on to their next cycle of team development.

THE FATE OF the USA Basketball Men's National Team changed forever on April 7, 1989. FIBA, the International Basketball Federation, overturned its rule: NBA players could now participate in international events, including the Olympics. Soon, the Dream Team was born. For a shining moment in time, Michael Jordan, Charles Barkley, Larry Bird, Karl Malone, Magic Johnson, and others were all on the same team. It's no wonder their closest game was against Puerto Rico, where they won with a 38-point lead (119 to 81), and we're pretty sure they eased up in the second half in the name of sportsmanship.

After that, the gold was considered a lost cause—unless you were Team USA. How could anyone possibly compete against the "best of the best"? That is, until 2004 in Athens.

The 2004 USA men's national basketball team had the talent, but it wasn't a team. In some ways, it was doomed from the start. Several players declined invitations, concerned that it was the first Olympics since the 9/11 bombings. Head coach Larry Brown preferred veteran players; the oldest player was 28. And he was attached to a particular style of play that diverted focus away from winning. The backcourt was led by Stephon Marbury and Allen Iverson, who were archrivals. Ego got in the way—they were often more concerned about what was best for their brand or shoe deal than for their country. On top of that, they had only a couple of weeks to play together before the tournament.

LeBron James reflected on his experience: "We had great basketball players but we didn't have the structure, and I think that's part of why we finished third."[1]

However, the USA men's national basketball team has taken home the gold every Olympics since, but we'll save the rest of that story for later. First, let's explore some of the telltale themes present in dysfunctional teams.

CULPRITS OF DYSFUNCTIONAL TEAMS

We are sure you've been a part of a dysfunctional team at some point in your life—whether that was a school project, a committee, or a work team. (Think about your spouse's or coworkers' complaints if you've been lucky enough to steer clear.)

When we asked our remote experts about the culprits of dysfunctional teams, a couple of themes surfaced: a lack of trust, ineffective communication, a lack of self-awareness, the inability to prioritize high-value work, and ineffective management. (Which ties nicely into one of Ali's favorite leadership books, Patrick Lencioni's *The Five Dysfunctions of a Team*.[2])

Specific to a remote environment, Rachel Korb, head of people and culture at Uizard, said, "Trust enables autonomy, collaboration, effective management, job performance, and engagement."

On ineffective communication, she went further, sharing: "This can come in many forms, from lack of transparency in decision-making and information sharing to assuming you understand what a team member is saying across high- and low-context cultures."

All of these create dysfunction in a team that eventually will bubble up. As we will explore in this chapter, the key to a successful team is to lean into the conflict and work to resolve it effectively, not to let it simmer and solidify into a culture of dysfunction.

❓ REFLECTION QUESTIONS

1. What's the main culprit you've witnessed on dysfunctional teams?

2. How have you seen high-performing teams navigate around that culprit?

THE FIVE STAGES OF TEAM DEVELOPMENT

Bruce Tuckman's seminal 1965 work "Developmental Sequence in Small Groups" introduced the world to the first four stages of team development: forming, storming, norming, and performing.[3] A decade later, Tuckman and Mary Ann Jensen conducted a follow-up review, where they added a fifth stage of development: adjourning.[4] This framework helped organizations see that a team is not a static entity but a living, breathing, incredibly human system.

Ali first studied Tuckman in university as a wee organizational behavior undergrad and later applied it at DuckDuckGo. To support a company-wide organizational redesign, Ali analyzed how a matrix organization[5] would work in a remote environment and supported the CEO and other stakeholders in the implementation.

DuckDuckGo grouped people into objective-based teams (e.g., short-lived teams supporting specific projects) and functional-based teams (e.g., long-term teams that act as a home base determined by core skill set). Case in point, Ali sat on an objective-based team to launch inclusive hiring and interview practices, but her functional-based team remained People Ops.

Other remote companies use similar structures, like Doist, with permanent and short-term "Squads" and "Crews." At Basecamp, they form new teams every six weeks for a product cycle, they take two weeks to breathe, and then a new team is formed.[6]

Tuckman's Five Stages of Team Development apply to both project teams and longer-term functional teams, though the length of each stage may vary. For example, a team at Basecamp may cycle through all five stages in six weeks, while a functional accounting team at a Fortune 500 company may be in the performing stages for years—at least until a new member joins or leaves the team.

We firmly believe that to perform as a remote team, you must experience the entire journey. Each phase cultivates the culture of the team. While it's human nature to want to skip past storming, your team will learn critical lessons during that stage. As your team completes each stage, you'll accumulate shared experiences, rituals, artifacts, expected behaviors, and language to help your team feel more like a "we" than a collection of "me's."

The result? By the end of this chapter, you will have a Team Charter that will act as a living, breathing contract to help your team stay on the same page even when they are not working in the same office (or continent).

Stage One: Forming

Forming is an act of creation. As a manager, you need to connect the dots for your team: Why is each person on the team? Why have you been tasked to work together? What are your shared goals?

Interestingly, the forming stage does not happen just once. A new team forms anytime someone is added to or removed from a team. This also applies to the same group of people coming together again for a new purpose.

From Akshay Kapur's vantage point, he's seen three types of formation: a team where everyone is new, an established team with a new manager, and an established manager getting one or more new members of the team.

While we think that pretty much covers it, we will add one more to Akshay's list: an established manager with a completely new team. In that scenario, the managers may have inroads with the broader organization but must establish trust with their direct team.

As a manager, you'll likely come back to the forming stage a few times, either when someone joins or leaves the team or as objectives change.

For example, Mike McNair described a project he worked on at L-3 Communications. His team was in the norming stage when the customer added a follow-on contract, new funding, and more requirements. That brought them back to the forming stage again.

According to Mike, "We had to look at our personnel assignments, schedules, and overall budget to ensure that we could get both projects done in parallel." Essentially, because the project's scope and goals changed, the raison d'être (that's "reason for being" in French, a subtle wink to our travel days) for the team also changed.

What's Unique about Remote

For a remote team, your coworkers will likely not sit next to you, nor will you be able to rely on subtle cues—like popping by their cubicle—to know what's going on. They might not even sit in the same time zone, let alone country.

In the Brady Bunch gallery view of video calls, you may see them only as legless humans for a while. (That's always Tam's big reveal at offsites. She's six-foot-one.) It may be hard to feel like a team with this physical distance unless you have a strong sense of purpose or togetherness.

Therefore, you'll need to be more intentional when coming together as a team and provide context. You will want to clearly state the team's goal, purpose, and vision—even though employees may not identify with it until norming begins!

You'll want to introduce the RW Collaboration Kickoff and RW User Guide during the forming stage. But remember, this level of getting to know each other requires a safe space and level of psychological safety—digitally. As a manager, use your facilitation skills to create a container where everyone feels comfortable sharing as much (or as little) about themselves as they want and establish clear points where team members can jump in and contribute.

You can use the two team-building activities that follow to support you through the forming stage. We also recommend that you have each team member share their RW User Guide and make the guides digitally accessible to the whole team so that individuals can work through work-style similarities and differences.

⚒ HOW-TO: Share Your Story

This exercise is an "ask me anything"-style introduction for team-mates to take turns on the center stage (or with Zoom's Spotlight feature).

Let each person on your team share a short introduction, which can cover their personal or professional journey, depending on the employee's comfort level. The catch? They should not mention their previous job titles or companies.

This peels back the surface-level judgments and allows employees to share what is important to them about their experiences. After their introductions, open the floor to the others and give the rest of the team a few minutes to ask "story" questions: who, what, when, where, and why (those 5Ws again). Here are two examples:

- What has been the biggest influence in your professional journey?

- Who is someone you would want to cowork with, living or dead, real or imaginary?

Pro Tips

- As a manager, you'll likely want to go first to be a role model and break the ice.
- This is a great activity for a company retreat where each employee gets the hot seat for one meal throughout a weekly offsite.
- For teammates who might be more shy or introverted, you may want to give them a heads-up before the activity so that they can prepare their story in advance. You can also do the entire activity asynchro-nously by posting intros and follow-up questions in a tool like Slack.
- Ensure safety by setting some limitations on what types of questions are appropriate based on the company's culture, and empower your employees to decline any questions they do not feel comfortable answering.

🔍 SPOTLIGHT STORY: Icebreakers IRL

Hilary Callaghan, an HR consultant and recruiter, recommended a similar exercise that she's seen used by Indigenous Australians, where "you talk about what got you here today, what land you're on, and where your family is from." According to Hilary, the activity transforms people from two-dimensional to three-dimensional beings and creates a foundation for sharing. She recommends starting with more straightforward questions and then moving to deeper questions after building trust.

Likewise, Mario Giulio Bertorelli, cofounder of Atium.app, a remote team-building platform, told us that the most popular icebreaker game on their platform is Fact Bucket. The rules are simple: Everyone submits a fact about themselves related to a question or a theme. Once the facts are submitted, each team member guesses which fact belongs to whom. It takes 10 minutes, and there are no distractions or call lag in this virtual version. According to Mario, "It's a very simple but powerful intervention." Mario said that asking a question like "Share a mistake you made last week at work" can foster a sense of vulnerability and psychological safety.

🔨 HOW-TO: RW Team Mission Statement

This brainstorming activity will help you cocreate your team's mission statement and help individuals identify with a higher purpose.

While many variations of this activity exist, we suggest a version that allows for individual asynchronous reflection time and a live or synchronous debrief—enabling your team to practice using different communication styles and online collaboration tools. Plus, it provides an equal playing field for the variety of communicators and learners on the team.

To start, pose a question such as, what does successfully achieving our goals as a team look like? Ask each team member to reflect and then submit their answer asynchronously to the question.

Put on your pattern-finding hat and pull out common themes across the team's answers. For an engineering team, achieving that goal may mean maintaining high standards in code reviews. For a People Operations team, that might mean creating a highly engaging place in which to work. You'll want to highlight any themes related to who, what, and why.

Next, you'll want to drill down to the specifics: "What actions make up our work, and how do they make an impact?"

Your final mission statement will answer those two questions in a succinct and unique way. For example, a team of site-reliability engineers may have this mission: "Harness our time-zone coverage worldwide to swiftly and accurately resolve issues, creating a seamless online experience for our users and internal teammates."

Pro Tips

- You can use tools like Mentimeter or MURAL to make the activity more visual and interactive.
- Be aware of "mission statement burnout." How often have you done a similar exercise and then felt like everyone forgot the following week? Your job as a manager is to ensure that this becomes a living, breathing document that guides your team's path. It needs a proper room in your Digital House, or else it's merely collecting virtual dust on a digital shelf (don't worry if that reference goes over your head; we will explain Digital House in the next chapter).

Stage Two: Storming

During this stage, individuals will start seeing themselves as part of the team (yay!); however, they may still be acting as individuals. Conflict will naturally arise from tension related to communication styles, work-style preferences, ways to approach problems and tasks, and previous work experience.

It is normal to want to skip over this stage and get to the good stuff, but if there's no conflict, it's likely a red flag. It could be a sign of fear or a lack of engagement. Perhaps team members have been punished in the past for speaking up or rocking the proverbial boat.

Your job as a manager is to identify moments of healthy storming (task friction) versus dysfunctional storming (people friction). You'll want to embrace task friction and develop behavioral norms to debate respectfully. Alternatively, you'll want to resolve people friction before it poisons relationships and creates a toxic work environment.

As Darcy Boles aptly said, "Collaboration often gets mistaken for consensus, but actually taking the time and energy to survey the team, talk to a lot of individuals, and see what the common themes are—that's what makes people feel like they belong."

As a manager, you must guide your team through the storm. It's high stakes. It's the make-or-break point for your team's future success. Sally Thornton, CEO and founder of Forshay Consulting, compares this stage to an organ transplant. She says it is like "adding a new organ to a body. You don't want the rejection. You've got to figure out how to make it beneficial and work on all sides."

So while some conflict at this stage is inevitable, it is important to uncover the root cause of the conflict and use the differences to explore what new norms you can build as a team.

What's Unique about Remote

What's a storm like on the waves of the internet with everyone in their own boat (or laptop, in this case)? Well, first, a conflict-avoidant team can hide behind their screens (literally and figuratively). This might prolong the storming stage, and in general, it's harder to see people's personality quirks asynchronously unless they are quite expressive with emoji use.

Common remote work tensions include preferences around asynchronous versus synchronous communication. You'll also start seeing the differences between employees who are more comfortable or experienced with remote work. They often crave more autonomy and resist the pull to be on back-to-back Zoom calls throughout the day while being more skilled in documenting their work processes.

Tam experienced this conflict after moving from a remote-first company back to a traditional work environment. When the pandemic hit, she expected remote working to reflect her experience at Automattic, but instead, she witnessed firsthand an emotional shock followed by growing pains and endless Zoom calls, which inspired the need for this book.

Tam struggled because as a new member of the team, she didn't have the clout to influence the organization. When she tried to explain how remote work could be completely different, it was met with blank stares and comments about Zoom backgrounds and ice-breakers. Rightfully so. They had never swum in that water, so it was hard to visualize how it could be different. It felt like explaining to a fish what it would be like to walk.

Push came to shove when Tam found herself on a project where the norm was three-to-four-hour-long team Zoom calls every day for brainstorming and collaboration. Her skillset differed from those on her team, as did her tasks. While her colleagues brainstormed novel marketing ideas, she needed to create an in-depth financial forecast and wanted time to analyze market data. When she requested to skip some of the calls to do her work instead, she came across as not being a team player. She learned that the conflict was not in fact personal; it was because of a difference of opinion on how to approach getting the work done. A classic storming conflict among a team with varying levels of remote work experience and autonomous skill sets.

A story like Tam's is not unfamiliar to Julie Armendariz, who has worked in HR for various companies, from those with strong office cultures to the leading remote "gold star" example, GitLab. Most recently, she worked at Hubspot, which migrated to a hybrid environment during the pandemic. She has seen storming in all environments throughout her career. Julie was able to sum up five aspects that were particularly unique to remote cultures:

- **Trust:** You need to be more intentional to create a genuine relationship remotely. "Until then, you have not earned that right or trust as a manager. You can't speak truth into someone else's life."

- **Timing:** It can take longer to resolve conflict. If the manager waits to talk to each team member in their prescheduled one-on-ones, it can take several days or weeks before the manager has connected with everyone involved. The manager can't walk down the hall in an office and talk to everyone right away.

- **Out of sight, out of mind:** "It can be easier to avoid conflict remotely because you're not going to run into that person in the hallway or break room. You delay addressing it right now because you're only going to run into them on a Zoom call." Sometimes that can be good, like when you need a cooling-off period. Still, Julie often sees it drag the conflict out.

- **Silence:** Beware of common phrases like "Silence is golden" or "No news is good news." Silence can signal a problem, like disengagement, burnout, or being scared to say what's really going on. Often managers feel blindsided when things blow up overnight, but in reality, tension was simmering until it exploded.

- **Follow-up:** Managers may assume that a conflict is resolved, but you can only know this through thoughtful check-ins. "When resolving conflict, the goal is to make something markedly better (resolve it), not just Band-Aid it."

These points suggest the need for a proactive plan to create space for issues to be heard, conflicts to be discussed, and resolutions to be made when working remotely.

🔍 SPOTLIGHT STORY: Storming Subcultures

Sometimes conflict expands beyond individuals or task friction. Let's dive into two stories: one about cultural friction and the other about functional friction.

Jason Morwick is the head of remote-first for Cactus Communications, a scientific translation company headquartered in India, with a presence in Japan, Korea, China, Denmark, and the United States.

When asked about friction, Jason recalled how cultural differences played a role in their marketing team's evolution, with team members in India and Japan. There's a three-and-a-half-hour time difference, and the Indian team prefers later working hours, while Japan keeps more traditional working hours.

You might guess where this story is headed. The India team kept scheduling late-afternoon meetings, which was well into the night for their Japanese colleagues. Rather than push back, the Japanese team kept with their cultural norms and said yes. It's considered inappropriate to decline a meeting. From Jason's vantage point, he saw "people accommodating others almost against their will. It was the *opposite* of what they would want to do."

Cactus rolled out training on cultural differences to combat this cultural friction and developed guidelines for setting personal boundaries (it's OK to decline a 10 p.m. meeting). Still, Jason finds that ultimately behavior change comes down to one thing: the expectations and norms set by leaders.

It doesn't always have to be cultural differences creating tension. Sometimes subcultures stem from role differences. Mike McNair, a remote aerospace VP at SAE ITC, believes that every project has its subcultures leading to friction. However, that can also lead to innovation.

In aerospace, Mike often sees a divide between engineering staff (who work remotely on their computers) and maintenance staff (on the ground next to the aircraft). "There's a lot of finger-pointing." Engineers will rebuke maintenance staff for not following their specifications, while maintenance folks will rebut that it doesn't work that way.

Knowing this tension, Mike and his project team developed a unique work-around for a highly sensitive handheld detector. They knew there was no way for his engineering team to be on the ground with the detector, so they set up a 1-800 number that they staffed 24/7 to troubleshoot any problems. When the time came for the person on the ground to use the detector, one of Mike's colleagues guided them step-by-step (without any finger-pointing!).

These stories show the importance of making it through the storming phase and the lessons that can be learned.

Stage Three: Norming

Phew, you're norming! We assume you're exhaling a sigh of relief if you're anything like us! *Finally*, the team is acting like a *real* team, and a unique culture is budding. Individuals see that they are more effective together than they are as individuals. As much as we dislike the word *synergy*, there's some 1 + 1 = 3 action going on now.

At this stage, you'll want to remind everyone of your RW Team Mission Statement and recognize the growing achievements as a unit (even if still in infancy at the moment). While still implicit, a shared vocabulary, rituals, and experiences bond the team—bolstering the Team Mission and subculture.

What's Unique about Remote

When colocated, you'll notice signs of norming when looking around the office. Team members chat in the hallways, body language looks more relaxed, and there are group celebrations for birthdays and other special events. These moments are often confused with the culture of a team. In the office, you'll find teams fixating on proxies for work—such as when people arrive at the office, who stays the latest, who appears to be working the hardest, and whether lunch is eaten out or at the desk.

In remote, norming is focused on standard operating behaviors (e.g., the actions that are rewarded and accepted by others), though the signals look different remotely. Rather than only looking for physical cues, you'll want to hone in more on the digital footprint left by the team. There will be remote best practice repetition without constant reminders: the daily stand-up meeting in Slack, tracking progress in a project management system, or adding documentation to the suitable digital space.

When norming, the team can work autonomously and get things done—on time. Individuals are more explicit about what they are working on and deadlines—actually following through on their word. A remote norm for Tam's partnerships team at Automattic was writing up meeting notes within 24 to 48 hours of a meeting and posting them internally.

During this stage, you'll also need to make an effort as a manager to help team members connect personally, given that there are fewer opportunities for spontaneous encounters and conversations.

⚒ HOW-TO: RW Team Charter

Now that you're witnessing norming behaviors across your team, you'll want to codify them. Think of the RW Team Charter as your team's North Star—it defines your team's direction while also explicitly stating boundaries. That is the ultimate goal and final artifact of the RW Team Charter.

It can be useful to run a team workshop to develop your RW Team Charter. However, think of the outcome as an MVP (minimum viable product) that you can continue building and refining over time, especially in the next stage, performing.

Once again, you'll want to spend time reflecting independently before coming together as a team (a remote working theme!).

Before building your RW Team Charter, it is important to allow time for the team to reflect on the following questions independently and then come together as a team, similar to the RW Team Mission Statement activity. (You'll notice that this is a common theme for remote working!)

We recommend that you start by independently answering the following questions and then come together live in a workshop, either on video or in person, to finalize norms for each topic (e.g., Team Goals,[7] Learning Opportunities). You can document each norm using the template at the end of this chapter or create your own.

Team Goals

1. How should we measure our success as a team this year?

2. What's one achievable goal? What's one stretch goal?

3. What would it look like if we reached these goals?

Learning Opportunities

1. What functional skills can we up-level this year?

2. How can we learn together as a team?

Meetings

1. When and why should we have synchronous (i.e., real-time) meetings?

2. How often should these be? How long? When is attendance optional?

3. What should be our meeting protocols? (Be as specific as possible
   —e.g., start the first five minutes with banter, require cameras
   on/off, send out an agenda beforehand, or rotate facilitator and
   notetaker roles.)

Collaboration

1. What tools should we use to communicate?

2. Where should certain types of communication happen (e.g.,
   project management in Asana or email for external communication only)?

3. What communication norms should we follow (e.g., tone of
   voice or stand-up formats)?

4. How can we see what each other is working on? How (and how
   often) will we check in with each other? How can we ask for
   support?

5. Do we need core working hours or time-zone overlap?

Documentation

1. What types of information do we need to record and archive?

2. Where will that information be stored? How will it be shared?

3. Who is responsible for maintaining and organizing
   documentation?

Expectations

1. What do we expect from each other as teammates?

2. What standard operating behaviors make sense, given our goals
   and the tools available?

3. How do these expectations show up virtually?

4. What can we do to hold each other accountable?

Building Culture

1. What words, acronyms, or phrases do we use that an outsider may not understand?

2. What symbols or artifacts appear in our online space that are meaningful to us as a team?

3. What rituals do we want to prioritize as a team?

Pro Tips

- The RW Team Charter should change. Team members will come and go. Preferences will evolve. Some norms won't feel all that normal anymore. You'll want to repeat this process and edit the RW Team Charter whenever the team changes or during annual planning.

- One solution might not satisfy everyone. Try to incorporate "and" norms in those scenarios instead of "or" norms.

- Keep your general expectations to fewer than seven bullet points. Make it memorable!

- Use specific but straightforward language that everyone will understand.

- If you need to gut-check an expectation, test it out by asking, "Is this normal on our team?"

- Ensure that the RW Team Charter is well documented and preserved in your Digital House (coming up in the next chapter). It will be a vital artifact for onboarding new team members and resolving future conflicts.

Stage Four: Performing

When your team is performing, you can feel it. The team is motivated and competent. As a manager, you'll notice the team making more decisions without you, and the quality of their outputs is higher. The team is flourishing in ways you weren't even expecting. It's nice to watch (and take part) in the dance.

According to Mike McNair, who has an agile project management background, you may see your team "swarming" during the performing stage. For example, you may see small teams of two or three self-form to hyperfocus on a task or problem, like a pitch deck or a piece of code.

What's Unique about Remote

While you may not physically feel the team abuzz with energy, you'll witness the work momentum through the computer screen. Once your team is performing, your days will be filled more with skilled work and strategy and less with work-about-work (e.g., admin tasks).

Your team is excelling. Projects are moving forward. Frameworks are second nature. And feedback loops are well-oiled machines. However, in remote, these signs of success look different.

Rather than seeing your team packed in conference rooms collaborating on whiteboards, you'll see the team respecting one another's autonomy and collaborating asynchronously first. Brainstorming might happen through a shared Google Doc, on a tool like MURAL, or through simple surveys and polls on Slack.

As a manager, you feel more comfortable trusting your team to get their work done, even if you can't physically see them completing tasks as you could in an office. You've made room for team members to craft their workdays, which means they can play with their kids or go for a run in between tasks. You care more about outputs than inputs. The "utopia" described in chapter 1 is starting to feel real!

Now that the team is performing, you can invest in team culture, social cohesion, and career development. We believe that if you focus too early on culture, it may feel disingenuous and forced. Once you've laid a foundation of trust, you can shape and play with the fun aspects of remote culture.

🔍 SPOTLIGHT STORY: A Product Release Despite All Odds

Chase Warrington, the head of remote at Doist, clearly remembers a moment when their company came together against all odds. The stakes were high. They were releasing a brand-new version of their product, Twist. It was the most comprehensive rebuild in company history, matched by the most comprehensive marketing release launch.

Their marketing team lost three or four team members in the middle of the launch. Plus, their head of marketing left on maternity leave. Instead of giving in or giving up, the team persevered. Chase was in awe as he watched colleagues from around the world come together and make sacrifices. In many ways, their culture led the team to perform.

According to Chase, somewhat unapologetically, "Bonding is not being forced to Zoom happy hour or game night together. We're a team, not a family. . . . We all believe in the work, which is our culture. We believe in the company's mission and being open and transparent, both internally and externally."

Referring to the launch of Twist, he continued, "This beautiful thing came from it at the end. And so far, it has been super-successful. That's a proud moment for me."

Stage Five: Adjourning

No matter how high performing your team is now, it will end one day. If there is one constant in life, it's that everything is constantly changing and evolving.

Laïla von Alvensleben from MURAL has seen her fair share of adjourning. She joined the company in its infancy and has seen it grow and morph over time. "You have to learn how to adapt. Some people find it harder because they're attached to the way the company used to be. They might be nostalgic about the smallness and the intimacy of knowing everybody; now they realize that they can't be updated about what everybody is doing anymore. Letting go of how things used to be takes time."

We recommend that managers celebrate the accomplishments of the team and members. Rituals provide closure and prepare the team for what comes next.

It's also important to note that not all adjourning is wanted. For example, your team may be reassigned against your will. You may have to deliver the news of a layoff or decide that the person is not a fit for the organization.

Whether the decision is yours to make or made for you, there will be a swirl of emotions to consider: anxiety about the future, uncertainty, and nostalgia. It is important for you as a manager to understand how your team may process these emotions and create a safe space in which to share.

What's Unique about Remote

An office-based farewell might look like happy-hour drinks or a cake, but a remote farewell often happens over the internet. When you're adjourning from afar, you need to think creatively to deliver a similar experience online. You'll want to find your unique way to send off employees that aligns with the team culture you've built.

When Tam left Automattic, she posted her farewell on an internal community blog. Colleagues across the company left comments sharing memories and wishing her good luck. (She kept a PDF of the post.) Although all written communication, it felt deeply personal and touching—in some ways, more than a happy hour in-person would have been. That ritual marked her rite of passage from an Automattician to proud Automattic alum.

If the adjourning looks more like a tough conversation, it's natural to want to lean on eye contact and body language when delivering it in person. However, the same message over Zoom may feel less personal.

Ali recommends referring back to the RW User Guide and tailoring your approach to the individual employee in this scenario. Before starting the conversation, it's important to get micro buy-in before delivering the news. Create space and ask if it is a good moment to talk. Some people will want privacy to absorb the information and reflect before asking questions. Others will want the news delivered over a live video call to preserve the relational elements of the interaction. By customizing the delivery, you can still be supportive based on the unique needs of your team.

Now for the practical part of adjourning: offboarding. If your team has maintained good remote work hygiene, such as documentation, it should be easy for the leaving employee to pass on projects, files, and history to their replacement. A smooth handover will make it easier for the team to reorganize and shapeshift.

As in the circle of life (cue the *Lion King* song), you're then back at the beginning: forming.

🔧 HOW-TO: Postmortem

If your team is adjourning because you've completed a project, we recommend holding a postmortem reflective meeting with a debrief document on successes and lessons learned as the resulting artifact. Afterward, the project is officially completed.

During the postmortem meeting, the team should reflect on questions (a few ideas follow) and communally close out the project.

- Were we ahead of or behind on our projected milestones? Why?

- What specific feedback would you like to share about the team, individuals, processes, or work?

- Are there any outstanding action items or next steps? Do we need to consider a future iteration of the project?

- What was challenging about the project? What lessons can we learn from our failures?

- What were our wins? Who and/or what played a role in accomplishing these goals?

Try to be as constructive as possible. Rather than expecting perfection, find ways to celebrate the wins and learn from the mistakes.

⚒ HOW-TO: The Toast

If the team reaches the adjourning stage because of a voluntary departure, celebrate the individual leaving the team. Prompt the team to share a memory about the individual either live, via video, or in a written format. This could be a funny story, a memory of working together, or a compliment. Have the leaving person write back a memory or comment for each story shared.

Pro Tips

- Keep it a secret leading up to the toast. Tam still remembers her team incognito, recording silly videos and sweet farewells around the Google office for their manager. There were lots of laughs (and the manager teared up at the end!).
- Don't be afraid to try different media. At IDEO, designers created visual farewells in Figma and MURAL with clip art, photos, etc.

❓ REFLECTION QUESTIONS

1. At which stage is your team currently—forming, storming, norming, performing, or adjourning?

2. What has been the biggest challenge in managing this stage remotely?

3. What is one activity you will try with your team? Be specific and commit to a date and action plan!

PUTTING IT TOGETHER: THE TEAM CHARTER

Use the template below to design your RW Team Charter after completing the Team Charter Workshop during stage three: norming.

RW Team Charter Template

Team name: Functional or objective name.

Team mission statement: The result of the Team Mission (forming) activity.

Members of the team (and link to their RW User Guide): You may choose to have both a public-facing RW User Guide and one that is private between just the employee and the manager.

Team goals: List one or two goals you want to accomplish together.

Learning opportunities: List one or two competencies you can develop together as a team.

Meetings: Summarize the team norms for synchronous and asynchronous meetings. Make sure to include: purposes, cadence, roles, and protocol.

Communication tools: Summarize the tools that the team will use, and provide simple rules on how to engage with them.

General expectations: Recap the five to seven expectations that the team decided on during the Team Charter activity. These will be your standard operating behaviors. Refer back to this section and update it often.

Collaboration: Summarize the team's main ways to collaborate and support each other.

Documentation: Summarize how information will be stored, shared, and updated.

Words and symbols: Document important words and symbols unique to the team to create a shared vocabulary.

Team rituals: Codify and list important team rituals that will happen on a daily, weekly, and monthly basis.

> **? REFLECTION QUESTIONS**
>
> 1. What parts of the Team Charter were the easiest to fill in? Did your team already have subconscious norms for those parts?
>
> 2. What is one way the Team Charter would help your team work better together?

· · · · · ·

Wow! You must be exhausted. Grab a glass of water and celebrate your accomplishments! It has been quite the journey, from forming your team to performing your best and possibly embracing your adjournment. Not unlike our USA men's national basketball team, we must say. Ready to finish that story?

OK, remember where we started this chapter? Athens. 2004. A bronze medal. We know that never happened again (at least thus far), but why?

The USA men's national basketball team learned from their mistakes and eventually moved past the storms of 2004.

In the summer of 2005, Jerry Colangelo was named director of USA Basketball. He took a different approach. He gathered past Olympic coaches and athletes to reflect on their successes and lessons learned. (Quite the star-studded postmortem!) It served as an adjourning ritual that provided him the insight to form the 2008 Olympic team.

According to Jerry, when he kicked off the forming stage,

> [p]art of my strategy was I wanted to look at each player one-on-one, eyeball to eyeball. I told them, "We want to do something very special. And if you want to be part of it, I promise you it'll be one of the great experiences of your life. And, if you want to be part of this, you're going to have to do A, B, C, and D, in terms of commitment."[8]

Each player knew why they were on the team. They had clear expectations and team norms, which helped them perform successfully.

As you steward your team through the five stages of team development, we hope you take what you learned from this chapter, the defects of the 2004 Olympics, and the team's rebirth under Jerry Colangelo. The phoenix rises again.

Remember, the five stages are a framework. It's an excellent guidepost, but your reality may vary. You may find that there are cycles and iterations. You may go back to a previous phase or notice that two are occurring in parallel.

We don't expect you to enter your team meeting and announce, "Now that we've stormed, let's kick off norming." But as you continue to manage and pay attention to patterns across teams, you'll build an innate sense of where the team is and how you can lead the way.

♥ ALI'S ADVICE

This chapter is a lot. We know. Take a deep breath. You got this!

Remote work is most successful when intentional. Even if you're not actively thinking about it, your team will naturally go through these stages.

If this feels overwhelming to you, it can be helpful to identify which stage you are at. That's it. You don't have to do anything else.

If you want to take a baby step further, identify your stage and choose one thing to practice. Remember, you can always reread this chapter when you graduate to the next team stage.

☺ TAM'S TIPS

It's unrealistic to leapfrog from forming to performing, no matter the talent or length of time you've been at the organization. If you don't believe me, reread the story about the 2004 Olympic basketball team.

By building foundational understanding and allowing team members to voice potential conflict areas, you can ease the growing pains—both for yourself and for everyone else involved.

CHAPTER FIVE

Your Digital House

🎯 TL;DR

In this chapter, we will reframe documentation and introduce the concept of a "Digital House" as a schema to orient your team around the digital tools and resources you use at work.

At the end of this chapter, you'll be able to do the following:

✓ Remove yourself as the intermediary by reducing dependencies and removing unnecessary "work about work."

✓ Enable seamless collaboration by ensuring that everyone has easy access to the information needed to do their job.

✓ Eliminate confusion and frustration over when and what tools to use by creating simple "House Rules" that outline standard operating behaviors within your Digital House.

DID YOU KNOW that there is an organized competition every year for—wait for it—memory? Since 1991, mental athletes worldwide have gathered to see who can memorize the most in a set amount of time—from shuffled decks of cards to unpublished poems to strings of binary numbers.[1]

While we won't be asking you to memorize anything in this book (you can always refer back at any time, we promise), there's a hack that most memory champions rely on: the memory palace. Essentially, you visualize a familiar place, such as your house or neighborhood, and then you place the object you're trying to remember in the order of the rooms. If you're trying to remember a simple grocery list with milk, bread, and bananas, you might mentally place spilled milk in your hallway, a lounging loaf of bread on your couch, and a monkey eating bananas on your kitchen counter. The more outrageous, the better, says the memory champions.

This memory hack works because of a little thing called schemas: you've already recorded the layout of your house in your long-term memory. It's much easier to recall new information, like a grocery list, when connected to a schema that already exists in your long-term memory.

THE DIGITAL HOUSE METAPHOR

Now, let's apply this schema concept to work. We're sure you've heard about the importance of documentation in remote work, but what is documentation exactly? It is not just notes scribbled in your notebook or a record of meeting notes with action items. In remote, documentation is so much more. It's how people work together. It's how complex processes work. It's subtle work preferences. All of these add up to the point that documentation itself becomes a living, breathing member of the team.

But what type of documentation should be included? Where should it live? How is it created? These questions leave remote work managers stunned when starting their journeys—overwhelmed by trails of the information left every which way (or lack thereof).

It can all seem vague. That is until we sat down with Sara Robertson. She introduced us to the "Digital House" concept, and then it all clicked.

Once upon a time, when you worked in an office (and might still be today), you had a schema for what happens where, reinforced by physical cues. Meetings happened in the conference room. Emails were sent from your desk. Impromptu socialization occurred at the water cooler. And the receptionist at the front desk answered your questions, same as your direct report, three cubicles away.

As work transitioned away from the office and onto a screen, you probably noticed an information gap. Where is all the intel you would have picked up informally in the office? How can you keep track of everything now that it's spread across so many tools, documents, and new communication channels, like Slack? When a calendar invite shows both Google Hangout and Zoom links, which should you click?

With remote work, you need to find a way to navigate your virtual world—both for yourself and for your team—similar to how you would in an office. To do that, you need a new schema to orient your digital work life. We call it "your Digital House."

A Digital House, according to Sara, is where you work and where you get the information to do your work. It has "rooms" that hold specific types of information or documentation, like project management or team policies. "House Rules" promote behavioral norms within the Digital House.

The Benefits

While there is a lot of hype around cool tools for remote work, we believe it's essential to understand the *why* before deciding on the *how*. We promise that doing this work up front will save a lot of confusion down the road!

According to Asana's Anatomy of Work Report 2021, 60 percent of workers' time is spent on "work about work," such as communication, coordination, searching for information, switching between apps, chasing status updates, duplicating efforts, and changing priorities. Work about work eats into your time to do skilled work. Workers report spending only 26 percent of their time on work they were hired to do.[2]

Let's pause to make sure that sunk in: only a quarter of workers' time is spent on the job they were hired to do! Not only is work about work wasted effort, but it increases fatigue and reduces motivation.

A Digital House will cut you out as the go-between, a prime work-about-work role. We promise that's a good thing! It allows you and your team to do the work that matters most and use your skills.

Benefit #1: A Digital House Removes Dependencies

Although we've been working in a digital-first world for a while, sending emails and clacking away on computers, we still have not fully harnessed its power. What would it look like if we played to technology's strengths? What if we let technology do what it's best at: processing information? And let humans do what they're great at: making meaning of that information?

In remote, information should never be the gatekeeper. Anyone anytime should be able to access the information necessary to do their job. It's the key to unlocking the magic of remote work—remember those Five Levels of Autonomy?

You can do your job at night or during the day. You can do your assignment from Austin, Texas, or Melbourne, Australia. If you're sick, the engine keeps running. If someone leaves your team, you may miss them, but they will not become the "single source of failure" for a project.

As Mike McNair aptly said about the phenomenon of a single source of failure, "People don't leave their brains behind. All that's left is what they've documented."

We agree but acknowledge that it's not always practiced. Tam still remembers a colleague emailing her about how to use a spreadsheet model that she made a year after she left the company. Tam wonders how much smoother off-boarding and knowledge sharing would have been if they'd had a company-wide Digital House in place.

A good rule of thumb is to build your Digital House so that your team could still function if someone left or if you never had a synchronous meeting again. (Though we still encourage synchronous meetings and interactions, especially for trust building and brainstorming; more on that later.)

Benefit #2: A Digital House Increases Visibility and Transparency

When Tam joined Automattic in 2017, she was astounded by the visibility and transparency across the organization. Never before in her career had she had *this* level of access. Besides confidential HR information, nearly everything was made public internally—whether that be a top-secret product release or investment conversations.

Automattic was able to do this because it had reimagined the concept of the meeting to fit a fully distributed company. All conversations were held on internal blog posts and in the comments sections rather than in real-time video meetings on Zoom or chatting in Slack.

This information added up, and Tam felt like she had a superpower. She no longer had to ask a ton of questions or search around through rushed documentation and poorly kept tracking spreadsheets to decipher partnership history. Instead, Tam could simply search for the partner's name, such as Microsoft, and every post written since 2005 would pop up. She could even set alerts to see anytime a partner was mentioned—which was incredibly helpful in an organization with functional partnerships across product, ads, marketing, and design.

Tam remembers writing a presentation for their semiannual partnership meeting between executives at Automattic and Google and easily being able to detail every technical integration between the two companies over the previous decade. Through documentation, she could decipher what worked and what could have been better, which gave her ideas for improving the partnership going forward.

She could do this because Automattic's culture encouraged making decisions out in the open and reinforced behavioral norms of regular documentation to make the invisible visible. Tam can remember, now fondly, the time that Matt Mullenweg, the CEO, scolded her for keeping a separate Google Doc with working notes. Within minutes, she copied and pasted everything onto an internal blog. (She assumes all is OK, given that he wrote the foreword.)

Remote powerhouses like Doist, Oyster, Zapier, Basecamp, DuckDuckGo, GitLab, and Human Made follow the same school of thought.

For example, Siobhan McKeown, the COO of Human Made, said, "We share everything that's not HR. It's important in remote work because it plays into accountability. If you can see the company's numbers, you're a part of creating the profit margins. . . . It helps people feel connected. It stops people from feeling like they're isolated. People can see into the business. It makes them feel like a part of it, rather than itemized people."

Not only is documentation hygiene a great practice for knowledge management, but it can foster trust and inclusion. Rachel Korb of Uizard honed in on the need for everything to be "remote-first" (even if hybrid) to create a truly inclusive organization. "This means defaulting to async first, documenting everything, keeping real-time meetings to a minimum (scheduled to include the majority of time zones and recorded for those who can't make it). Key decisions are made online, so everyone is included. Performance is measured by results rather than hours worked. Processes and tools are designed to include all team members regardless of location. And people and information are equally accessible to all people."

🔎 SPOTLIGHT STORY: Making a Mental Map

Tam was known for a few things at Automattic. Besides being one of the few females in their annual "Tall-matticians" photos at their company offsite, she had a knack for connecting dots across the organization and never dropping the ball.

Words like *speed, responsiveness, diligence,* and *reliability* dominated her performance reviews, which would seem normal if Tam were organized by nature. But if you ask her parents, *organized* is the last word they would have used to describe her. Her room was always a mess when she was a kid (and to be honest, it still is), and half-finished art projects were scattered across the game room. You could find her in the house by the trail of items, like her backpack or water bottles, all left in her wake.

So how can both of these things be true? Well, Tam took a tip from the London Black Cab drivers. To become a cabbie, drivers need to pass the "Knowledge of London" test, which requires memorizing thousands of streets, landmarks, and routes in central London. It generally takes three to four years to study, and guess what—their brains change. The hippocampus enlarges, due to the vast amount of navigational knowledge.

Likewise, Tam made a mental map of Automattic so that she could visualize the company's inner workings. P2 (internal blogs) served as teams' knowledge bases (often with fun names, like Hogwarts), and each individual had an avatar or profile image. She formed a mental map with roads between teams that cross-posted within each other's knowledge bases. Landmarks became certain issues or topics that kept surfacing across the company, with familiar avatars attached.

This mental map came in handy while leading complicated cross-functional partnerships between Automattic (and its subsidiaries, like WooCommerce and Jetpack) and behemoths like Google and Amazon. It helped her keep track of dozens of integrations and touchpoints between the companies and the relevant stakeholders, from ad managers to developers to cloud specialists. All she needed was her mental map and internet access to remember who owned what and who needed to connect with whom.

Benefit #3: A Digital House Archives Team Identity

We love museums. There's something magical about walking through curated histories of our world, whether that's Francis Bacon's *Three Studies for Figures at the Base of a Crucifixion* in the Tate Modern (truly terrifying) or the fashion collection in the V&A and the Rosetta Stone at the British Museum across the Thames.

According to anthropologists, there are five tenets of culture: symbols, language, beliefs, values, and artifacts. And as a team, you'll be creating a subculture of your own that you'll want to archive and preserve.

As Sara Robertson, who initially coined "Digital House," told us, "The problem with digital is it's imaginary. There's nothing solid. There's nothing fixed. It's an idea in our heads, and it's pixels showing up on the screen. As humans, we crave having home and identity."

In digital, that place to belong can feel amiss. Likewise, there are no social cues. How are we expected to behave? Sara used the University of Edinburgh as an example. It's clear what students do where: they listen in lecture halls, have free-form conversations in the hallways, and socialize over a pint or two. This isn't by accident; it's quite intentional. When new students arrive, the university puts a lot of thought into Welcome Week, introducing students to shared history and behavioral norms.

At Hotjar, they dedicate the first few weeks for new employees to onboarding. According to Ken Weary, "Dropping someone straight into their work might be what they're hungry for, but it does not set them up for long-term success." Instead, the company uses a self-guided process in Trello boards to orient new hires to "the company, our history, core values, culture, org structure and other foundational aspects of the company."

With this in mind, as a manager, you'll want to think about your team's Digital House, not only as a way to share information but also as a cultural archive of all that your team was, is, and hopes to become. You can do this by creating artifacts, such as the RW Team Charter discussed in the last chapter, and discussing as a team which behaviors are acceptable. For example, casual conversations should happen in the #wtrclr (water cooler) Slack channel, and project management templates should be stored in the Library section of Notion.

> **❓ REFLECTION QUESTIONS**
>
> 1. How does your team struggle with information sharing and documentation?
> 2. How might a Digital House solve those challenges?

MOVING IN: WHAT TO BRING

Now that we've discussed the benefits of a Digital House, it's time to discuss the big moment: Move-In Day. We assume you're not coming empty-handed. Most likely, you already have software, documents, and systems that you've been using (or were assigned by your IT team).

Taking Inventory

We recommend auditing where all of these activities happen today—both within your team and cross-functionally across the organization.

You'll want to note all the tools you are using. Think of these as the "rooms" within your Digital House, such as the following:

- **Synchronous communication** (examples: Zoom, Slack, conference calls, retreats)

- **Asynchronous communication** (examples: Slack, Loom, email, Google Docs)

- **Project management** (examples: Google Docs, Asana, Monday, Notion, Doist, Trello)

- **Knowledge base** (examples: Coda, Notion, intranet, field guides)

- **Collaboration** (examples: MURAL, Miro, Google Docs, Figma)

- **Function-specific tools** (examples: Canva, GitHub, Photoshop)

You should also include tool-agnostic templates that support your work. Think of these items as the furniture, and determine which rooms they belong in:

- **Project management information** (examples: templates, README guides, trainings)

- **Team norms and policies** (examples: RW Team Charter, HR policies)

- **People management** (examples: RW User Guides, directories, trainings)

- **Culture** (examples: glossaries, FAQs)

Think through *all* the rooms and pieces of furniture you have and want to keep.

Tidying Up

Now comes the fun part: tidying up your Digital House.

We expect you'll find some room for improvements. For example, you may learn that your team uses several different platforms for videoconferencing or there's no clear rule around when to communicate via email or Slack. You may find that information that should be contained in RW User Guides is scattered piecemeal across your Digital House (like personal calendars that show working hours and employees' Slack bios listing their strengths and interests). As a team, harness your own inner Marie Kondo and decide what to keep and what to discard—thanking the tools, processes, and behaviors that no longer serve you.

✘ HOW-TO: Checklist for Streamlining Your Digital House

- ☐ **Audit** where all the work happens today.

- ☐ **Build** a list of needs for your team (assuming you are starting from scratch).

- ☐ **Compare** what works and what doesn't from your current tool set and the suggested rooms and furniture of your Digital House.

- ☐ **Decide** how to organize tasks, activities, and information in your Digital House going forward.

Of course, this might not be straightforward. In that case, we suggest prototyping a way of organizing for a set period of time and then coming back as a group and iterating.

Maintenance

Like a real house, your Digital House will need to be maintained. Therefore, develop good hygiene habits, like documenting, working in the open, and forgoing (or documenting) side conversations.

According to Ken Weary, "Our company and its culture is a living organism. There's always change happening across the company, and when something changes, it's very likely that the documentation also needs to change or be updated. . . . If we don't update, then the team will begin to see the documentation as outdated and stop using it."

You'll also want to create a field guide or README that outlines where everything lives in your Digital House, so that team members can quickly get the information they need.

🔎 SPOTLIGHT STORY: How Tools Can Change the Way You Work

If you search stock photos for "collaboration," you'll find images of teams gathered around meeting room tables with colorful sticky notes lining the walls. But what's the new mental model for collaboration in the remote world?

We spoke to Laïla von Alvensleben, the head of culture and collaboration at MURAL, to learn more about remote collaboration.

MURAL, at first glance, is a digital whiteboard with all the features you'd expect: sticky notes, diagrams, icons, digital markers, and even GIFs. But Laïla believes it's more. The tool is changing the way people work. "I see collaboration as an exchange of ideas to create something."

Bringing a digital whiteboard into your Digital House shifts old power dynamics. According to Laïla, "It's changing structures within companies, and it also democratizes ideas. It's more inclusive; as a canvas, anybody can come in and add their ideas. It's not the loudest person in the room, or the person who's standing by the physical whiteboard with a marker, who's going to take control of the flip chart."

The tools you select can reinforce (or negate) the behaviors you want to cultivate. How are your tools serving your goals? The next section will discuss how having explicit, intentional House Rules can make your tool set even more powerful.

HOUSE RULES: HOW TO ENGAGE

Now that you've sorted out *where* things live in your Digital House, it's time to think about *how* to engage within the Digital House.

House Rules are agreed-upon standards that inform behavior within your working team through a series of tools, templates, processes, and norms. You can document House Rules in your RW Team Charter as a reference.

While it may be tempting to create detailed rules about everything, it's a good *rule* of thumb for your House Rules to be few, easy to understand, and actionable.

Let's explore an illustrative example: team announcements.

Imagine you're the manager, and your team has started complaining about announcements. Announcements are being sent out willy-nilly—at all times, about all things, across all communication channels. Some people send a Slack message and tag "@all," sending noisy notifications regardless of time zone. You have been sending announcements by email, only to discover that several of your teammates rarely check their work email unless chatting with someone outside of the company.

You sit down and note your team's grievances. (Even the most minor things can add up!) Maybe you even observe what other teams do or read advice online. Feeling good about the direction forward, you create a list of House Rules to get this announcement problem under control ASAP and announce it, of course.

1. Announcements should only come from *you*, the manager, going forward.

2. If anyone has an announcement to make, they should create an Asana task and assign it to *you* by noon ET on the day of the announcement.

3. Announcements should have a descriptive title and a link to more-detailed information.

4. You will compile all the announcements and share at 1 p.m. Eastern time in a new #TeamAnnouncement channel in Slack, not tagging anyone.

5. Each announcement will have its own thread.

6. People should comment only within threads.

7. Emojis can be used to vote or take action on an announcement.

8. Announcements can be used for project updates, holidays, and company initiatives.

A week goes by, and still no improvement. The team still seems confused when you reference "House Rules" in the team meeting. Plus Slack and email are still a mess, with minor announcements throughout the day.

The problem? While the rules were actionable and specific, there were frankly too many of them and no buy-in from the rest of the team. A set of rules does *not* equal a behavioral change.

You decide to go back to the drawing board.

To create *simple* House Rules, it is crucial to clarify the intent (why is it important?) and the functionality (how will it work?).

In this scenario, you realize that it is vital to distinguish company, cross-functional, and team announcements.

You decide that company and cross-functional announcements should have the same House Rule. As a manager, you often have access to information that your team does not. Systematically sharing this information will keep employees in the loop of significant decisions and increase transparency and motivation.

Now that you've clarified your intent, it's time to think through the functionality. How should you share company and cross-functional announcements with your team? You know you want to reach employees quickly and have visibility on who has read the announcement.

Let's revise that simple House Rule:

1. For company or cross-functional announcements, I will post in our #Team-Announcements Slack channel, as needed, in written and video formats.

2. It will be pinned to the top of the channel until everyone has responded with a thumbs-up emoji that they have read the message.

3. All questions should be posted in the thread.

That's more like it. They follow the criteria: few, easy to understand, and actionable.

You then realize that announcements coming from the team often are on a few topics (availability, personal updates, and project management). Therefore, you can create House Rules to incorporate the announcement content into existing habits. Here are some examples:

- **Team availability:** Share in the "Team Meeting" tasks in Asana on Mondays. Block holidays or breaks longer than four hours in your calendar.

- **Personal updates:** Share asynchronously in the stand-up thread kicked off by you every Tuesday and Thursday in the #Team Slack channel.

- **Project management:** Share status updates weekly on Fridays (at a minimum) as a comment on the project task in Asana.

These simple House Rules will help your team work in predictable ways. They reinforce standard operating behaviors of culture, build trust, and remove the mental overhead of work about work. But remember, your job as a manager is to mirror the behaviors you want to see (and gently remind those not following the House Rules as they develop new habits).

Good guidelines should help, not hinder, your team's ability to perform. Jaclyn Rice Nelson from Tribe AI approaches guidelines with a question: "How can we make it easy for people to plug in?" Jaclyn has found that you're not cramping their style by giving them guidelines. "You're making it easier for them to do their best work."

🔍 SPOTLIGHT STORY: Automattic's Simple Rules

Remember how Tam started to create mental maps of where things lived digitally at Automattic? It wasn't just her visualization that kept things running smoothly. The entire company kept it simple by using their own product, the blog platform P2, as the main tool for communicating, sharing knowledge, and getting the work done. Even still, there were a few House Rules, according to Tam, that helped make Automatticians feel more at home when approaching their work. For example:

1. Slack is for quick, casual conversations, either work related, personal (vacation time), or conversational (workday banter and jokes). To prevent always-on behavior, they used "AFK" in their Slack statuses to indicate that they were "away from the keyboard" and would not be responding immediately.

2. P2 (internal blogs) is for official communication. It replaces both the meeting and email. Comments and likes serve as collaboration.

3. Email is for external use only (e.g., partnerships and sales teams).

4. Zoom is the preferred video call tool. If external facing and regularly taking Zoom calls with partners, work in a time zone with at least two hours that overlap in both Pacific time and Eastern time.

🛠 HOW-TO: Your Digital House in Action

Now that you have completed your audit, tidied up, and created House Rules, let's make it official! You can use the chart that follows to document your Digital House and share it as the final map with your team (table 5.1).

TABLE 5.1 RW Digital House Template

	WHERE IT HAPPENS (TOOLS)	WHAT WILL BE HOUSED THERE (TEMPLATES, INFORMATION, ETC.)	HOUSE RULES
Synchronous communication tool			
Asynchronous communication tool			
Project management tool			
Knowledge base			
Collaboration tools			
Functional-specific tools			

But it doesn't end there! Make sure you *follow* your own House Rules and continue to refine your Digital House going forward. (Plus, this Digital House chat is excellent practice for building your documentation muscles and summarizing final decisions for future reference.)

🔍 SPOTLIGHT STORY: Cody's Digital House at Zapier

When we asked Cody Jones of Zapier to describe their Digital House, he immediately commented on their culture. They love technology and tinkering. "Honestly, it's changing all the time. We love SaaS [software as a service], which means, unfortunately, we have every tool you could possibly imagine. We're getting better, though, using certain tools for certain jobs to be done."

Let's walk through Cody's Digital House at Zapier together.

Communication Tools

According to Cody, "Slack is how we do business. I do not use email. Slack is the backbone of our organization." They encourage everyone to use the public channels (cue transparency) instead of DMs (direct messages). They even set up x-company Slack channels with specific partners while working on a collaboration or integration.

Similar to Tam's experience at Automattic, Zapier uses a form of internal blogging called Async. "Async is where company decisions, Friday updates, and everything else you need to read are shared and commented on."

Project Management

Like all good tech companies, Zapier "dogfoods" their product called Zaps.[3] "A lot of our team meetings, rituals, documents, and documentation are through Zapier."

Cody especially likes to use Zaps to encourage organization, rituals, and norms within his team. He'll create a Zap to automatically make a new document with a specific template for a meeting. It will then notify his team on Slack, reminding them of the upcoming meeting and prompting the team to fill out the information in their assigned sections. On the day of the meeting, the Zap sends out the Zoom link and the document with the agenda. Everything is ready to go!

According to Cody, "Half of the battle is consistency in documentation. This automates it, so you don't have to worry about building the habit. The automated habit creates all the documented artifacts, and the artifacts save us tons of time in the future."

House Rules

Their norms have evolved since the early days. "Everything was on Async. You had to do your Friday update, and it could never be a video. No verbal anything. It was all written."

As for Slack, initially the rule was "Anything goes," but over time they added "specific norms for Slack on response times, what's appropriate versus what isn't, and DMs versus public."

And while this is how Cody's Digital House at Zapier looks today, it might have an extra room or a fresh coat of paint by the time this book is published.

Table 5.2 shows how Cody and his team could document their Digital House using the chart template:

TABLE 5.2 RW Digital House—Zapier Spotlight Story

	WHERE IT HAPPENS (TOOLS)	WHAT WILL BE "HOUSED" THERE (TEMPLATES, INFORMATION, ETC.)	HOUSE RULES
Synchronous communication tool	Zoom Krisp	Nothing is housed there. These tools are for synchronous calls.	Use Krisp to create a quiet environment, especially on external calls.
Asynchronous communication tool	Async (internal tool) Slack	Async: Company decisions and updates. Slack: Where the "work" gets done.	Updates are posted in Async on Fridays. Slack: Public channels by default.
Project management tool	Coda Slack Zapier	Coda: For meeting notes and information. Slack: For the work.	Create Zaps to automate whenever possible. Invite external collaborators to specific Slack channels .
Knowledge base	Coda Zapier	Prereads and meeting notices, as well as all documentation.	Document as you go using Zaps.
Collaboration tools	Google Docs Coda Async (internal tool)	Google Docs: Work-in-progress collaborations. Coda or Async: Final documentation.	Google Docs are considered work in progress.
Functional-specific tools	Copper CRM HubSpot Looker Zendesk	Copper CRM: Pipeline Hubspot: Client messaging. Looker: Analytics. Zendesk: Partner tickets.	Not shared.

Not only will this exercise help you share the information effectively, but also it will ensure that your Digital House doesn't have the digital equivalent of a leaky roof or broken plumbing.

We recommend that you revisit this chart quarterly to make sure the information is up-to-date and create a digital copy in your version of your team's knowledge base.

> **? REFLECTION QUESTIONS**
>
> 1. Are you lacking any tools in your Digital House? What will you use moving forward?
>
> 2. What is a new House Rule you can introduce for your favorite tool?

♥ ALI'S ADVICE

I am a big fan of "working out loud." Don't wait until you have a perfect rough draft before sharing publicly with your team. Create a first draft, share and ask for feedback, and then iterate within the tool.

Working in this public way is faster and prevents duplicated efforts and time wasted perfecting too early. There should be a "single source of truth"—not different copies for different people. That's one of the benefits of the Digital House: promoting transparency and collaboration.

☺ TAM'S TIPS

It can be a hassle to keep up with documentation. Instead, make documentation a part of your workflow.

For example, Ali and I do most of our project planning in Asana, using "tasks" to document meeting notes and "projects" to contain our projects (obviously). We write and plan workshops in Google Docs, using comments and version history to track changes.

Our work is de facto documented—which means we're not wasting time retyping notes—part of the beauty of asynchronous communication!

I specifically like a rule of thumb that Jason Morwick mentioned in his interview: You know your documentation game is on point when you can answer a colleague's question with a link where they can find the answer—already written.

CHAPTER SIX

Getting Things Done

🎯 TL;DR

In this chapter, we will reframe productivity for the remote manager by discussing how to manage your time, energy, and focus (and help your team do the same).

At the end of this chapter, you'll be able to do the following:

✓ Accomplish your goals faster by working in ways that play to your energy levels, setting top priorities, and focusing on outputs.

✓ Restructure your schedule and own your calendar to allow for more balance between creating and managing.

✓ Be super-focused when you are getting things done by streamlining decision-making; incorporating macro, meso, and micro breaks; and setting boundaries.

GROWING UP, Ali was good at math—so good that she attended a local community college for advanced algebra and calculus while still in high school. Therefore, when Ali went away to university to study business, a finance or accounting degree was the obvious choice. That is, until she learned that while the finance majors busied themselves with calculations and spreadsheets, the organizational behavior (OB) students were off playing games and going on team-building retreats. She immediately enrolled in as many OB classes as possible, a decision that changed the direction of her life.

And so Ali was genuinely thrilled to teach productivity workshops early in her career as a learning and development specialist, putting her degree and love of problem-solving to good use. Plus, Ali already considered herself an expert on time management. While colleagues struggled to get everything done, she often struggled with the opposite problem: finishing her work too fast. Her options weren't great; she could either take on extra work (with no raise) or attempt to look busy while stuck in the office—until she moved to remote!

Her productivity training contained the typical suspects: Stephen R. Covey's *Big Rocks* and Eisenhower's Urgent/Important Principle. And while she still believes in what she taught, Ali recognizes now that she was solving for the wrong variable. It was all based on a constraint that no longer needs to exist: how much work you can get done in the limited hours in an office.

After transitioning to remote, Ali learned that productivity is *not only* about time management through firsthand experience: an intense hiring sprint for software engineers. Her work seemed to take hours when she triaged résumés and scheduled interviews in the morning. However, when Ali settled in to do the same work after dinner, snuggled up on the sofa with good music and a cup of tea, she worked faster. Finally, she could focus and get into a flow state and ultimately finish the same workload in drastically less time with better results. Ali up-leveled her productivity game by simply changing the *time of day*. (Plus it meant she could make her favorite late-morning yoga class.)

That was when it clicked: Productivity is more than task lists, the Pomodoro Technique, and fancy software. What if, all along, teams have been defining it wrong for the modern workforce?

We went back to first principles—the dictionary—and found *productivity* aptly defined as "the quality, state, or fact of being able to generate, create, enhance, or bring forth goods and services."

Fundamentally, productivity is the ability to do what you set out to do, and therefore it also entails creating an environment ripe for you to produce your best work.

With all of this in mind, we decided to go straight to the scientific source on productivity: Sahar Yousef, PhD, a cognitive neuroscientist and lecturer at UC Berkeley's Haas School of Business who has made studying human performance her life's work.

As Tam sat down (virtually of course) with Sahar, she quickly learned what made Sahar tick: "My area of expertise is really how do we make humans better? How do we increase attention span? . . . If I can help make individuals, teams, and organizations just a little bit more productive, and more physically and mentally well, then I can help propel humanity forward in my small way."

It's with this lens that Sahar walks into the modern workplace; rather than seeing people, she sees brains. And she's been shocked to discover how little organizations and leaders understand about the human brain, considering that a company is really just a collection of many highly educated brains.

How can you better use your brain and the brains of those you manage? It requires reframing. Every morning, you wake up with three essential resources for human productivity: energy, time, and focus.

One of the key culprits of productivity burn? Multitasking. As Sahar pointed out, "The human brain is not designed to multitask; we are focus machines. There is no such thing as multitasking, or doing two cognitively demanding tasks at the exact same time." Instead, we are either doing both tasks poorly or rapidly context-switching.

Mike McNair of SAE ITC likens the idea of multitasking to a computer operating system:

> We've all experienced that lag when we have too many windows open, browser tabs going, and apps running. Behind the scenes, the computer operating system is asking, "Which of these apps should I be running right now?" It is trying to give them all equal time to get their jobs done. It's similar to people. If people don't manage their time well, they can get into a mode where they're spending all of their time figuring out what they should be doing instead of getting something done.

According to Mike, this can be especially tricky in a remote context without open communication. "People can spend a lot of time second-guessing themselves if they don't have someone to bounce ideas off of."

And while it can feel good to switch contexts, zipping from Slack messages to emails to social media, each giving us a hit of dopamine, there's a real cost to switching that we pay for in both time and energy. It takes us longer to do the same tasks, and we are more likely to make mistakes.

❓ REFLECTION QUESTIONS

1. How will you inspire and protect your team's most precious resources?

2. How can you limit the energy and time you spend multitasking?

MANAGING YOUR ENERGY

Ali has been living the mantra of managing energy, not time, ever since her experiment of nighttime résumé reading. Likewise, we found that other remote experts learned the same lessons through trial and error.

When Steph Yiu of WordPress VIP first started working remotely, she struggled. "It was such a hard transition for me. It took me about two years to get the hang of it. Until then, I was pretty depressed or anxious." Since then, she's led 100-person remote teams. Her secret? Knowing the factors that help her thrive. "Knowing what I need, what hours I'm most productive, and how I learn best allows me to be really dynamic in a remote environment."

Each person has their rhythms and biological patterns, and when you work following your natural energy, not against it, you can get more done in less time. (And justify that afternoon catnap you've had your eye on.)

A McKinsey study found that "top executives report being five times more productive during their peak performance hours in the day—yet only 5% of them report being in a state of deep engagement during this time."[1] The takeaway? Even if you know when you are most productive, you need to use that time wisely. This can be a trap when you are working in a nine-to-five routine and aimlessly responding to emails or sitting in meetings; instead, we recommend intentionally working on the most mentally challenging work during your peak performance hours. This aligns with what we heard in our remote work expert interviews. Colloquially, folks felt four times more productive when working on a schedule aligned with their energy levels. If you're trying to complete a task with low energy, it may take hours. If you're in a flow state, it may take minutes. Science supports this phenomenon. We each have a chronotype, a circadian typology that differentiates our general alertness in the morning or evening.

Dr. Sahar Yousef's lab, Becoming Superhuman, profiles the three core chronotypes: Type 1: AM-Shifted, Type 2: Bi-phasic, and Type 3: PM-Shifted (table 6.1).[2,3]

According to Sahar, "You should experiment with specific times for certain activities, but the general rule is to do your analytical work during your peak, your administrative work during your dip, and your creative work during your recovery."

Taking Sahar's chronotype quiz was a relief for Tam, finally having data to confirm what she always knew: she is a night owl. She now feels compassion for her bleary-eyed self, taking the first flight out as a management consultant and dreading her 6 a.m. alarm to catch the bus down to Mountain View, hoping to miss the traffic.

TABLE 6.1 Becoming Superhuman: Three Core Chronotype Profiles

TYPE 1: AM-SHIFTED (20–25% OF THE POPULATION)	TYPE 2: BI-PHASIC (50% OF THE POPULATION)	TYPE 3: PM-SHIFTED (20% OF THE POPULATION)
AM-Shifted people feel most alive in the morning. They can complete a massive amount of work before lunch! In the evening, these types feel drained.	Bi-phasic people are neither morning people nor night people but rather thrive in two peaks.	PM-Shifted people do their best work after hours into the wee hours of the night. Their first peak starts at 5 p.m. when traditional offices are closing for the day.
Peak focus (for analytical work): 7:00–11:00 a.m.	**Peak focus (for analytical work):** 9:00 a.m.–1:00 p.m.	*Notice that energy recovery comes before peak focus for PM-Shifted.*
Energy dip (for administrative work): 11:00 a.m.–2:00 p.m.	**Energy dip (for administrative work):** 1:00–4:00 p.m.	**Energy recovery (for creative work):** 10:00 a.m.–4:00 p.m.
Energy recovery (for creative work): 2:00–6:00 p.m.	**Energy recovery (for creative work):** 4:00–9:00 p.m.	**Energy dip (for administrative work):** 4:00–6:00 p.m.
Optimal sleep window: 9:00 p.m.–6:00 a.m.	**Optimal sleep window:** 11:00 p.m.–8:00 a.m.	**Peak focus (for analytical work):** 6:00–10:00 p.m.
		Optimal sleep window: 1:00–10:00 a.m.

Note: For more depth, take the Biological Chronotype Assessment from Dr. Sahar Yousef's lab: mychronotype.com/. Use code REMOTEWORKS for 50% off.

Tam's world changed when she discovered remote work and synced her schedule with her energy. Her first stop as a digital nomad was Lisbon, Portugal, where she'd wake up at 10 a.m., work at a café down the street, then take a long walk or visit a museum in the afternoon. She'd finish assignments before dinner and take a few late-evening calls with external partners starting their days in Silicon Valley.

But you might be thinking, I don't totally fit into one category. (We see you, you special snowflake.) That is OK too! The important thing to take away is that you naturally have peaks and flows in your energy levels throughout the day, and with remote work you have the power to listen to them and work with them instead of trying to fight against them and conform to one style.

And we promise that different types can work together! Tam is a tried-and-true PM-Shifted night owl; and, as Ali jokes, she's a solid late-afternoon person and, per her story, reviews candidate résumés best outside of "normal work hours." We make it work by using asynchronous communication, flexible schedules, and time zone hacks. Calls at 11 a.m. Eastern time for Tam and 5 p.m. Central European time for Ali are optimal for both parties to brainstorm.

Energy Tracking

Besides your natural cycles, other factors can influence your energy level, such as who you are working with and your physical environment. For example, do you need to be alone in your "cave" or at a bustling café or coworking space?

Or you might find yourself in flow during certain activities. Ali loves leading webinars and sharing ideas on podcasts, and Tam thrives when interviewing people and connecting dots across interdisciplinary subjects. These activities leave us feeling more energized.

While you likely have a hunch about your energy peaks and dips, some aspects are less obvious, especially if you have trained your whole adult life to work in a nine-to-five office environment. We recommend that you take it a step further and track your energy for a week.

✎ EXERCISE: RW Energy Tracker

The RW Energy Tracker is a diary study to help you identify and understand your biggest energy boosters and drainers to make changes to optimize your workflow.

Anytime you complete a task for work or in your personal life (e.g., cleaning out your in-box), or an event happens (e.g., going to boxing class or leading a project-kickoff meeting), take a minute to jot down the before-and-after impact. You can do this in a journal or use our custom-made RW Energy Tracker (grab your copy from remoteworksbook.com). Ideally, you'll want to track at least two to three events per day—a mix of work and personal.

At the end of the seven days, review your responses and see what trends you're noticing. Take a moment to reflect on the following questions:

- What boosts my energy?

- What drains my energy?

- What types of tasks could be eliminated without consequence?

Now that you have a better sense of your energy, it is time to make some decisions and take action! How can you prototype some changes based on what you learned? Not an early bird? Save your heads-down tasks for later in the afternoon. Have an energy boost after boxing class? Perhaps you can use that energy to knock out focused work afterward.

Pro Tips

- While this is a great solo activity to gain more self-awareness of how you like to work, it is also a fantastic team-building activity to see similarities and differences at the team level.
- As you figure out your energy patterns using the RW Energy Tracker, codify them in your RW User Guide and RW Team Contract. Think of yourself as a designer of your workweek. The more you learn about yourself, the more you can attune your week to your rhythms.

🔍 SPOTLIGHT STORY: An Energy-Optimized Week with Steph Yiu

Remember Steph, the WordPress VIP who initially struggled to find her rhythm working remotely? After learning about managing her energy, she restructured her workflow to get more done. How did she do it? By embracing her chronotypes, energy boosters, and energy drainers.

Flexing to Her Early-Bird Chronotype

"For me, morning time is very precious. I try not to schedule any calls in the morning as much as possible. That's my focus time."

Balancing Draining Work

"I'm conscious of how I absorb information. I am 100 percent an auditory learner. I love consuming information through podcasts. Suppose I need to consume things in a written format. In that case, I try to carve out time and limit the amount on any given day."

Scheduling for Energy Management

1. **Get the Ball Rolling Mondays and Tuesdays:** Steph schedules all of her normal cogs-in-the-wheel work for the first half of the

week, such as team stand-ups and regular one-on-ones with her direct reports.

2. **Deep Work Wednesdays:** Steph avoids calls on Wednesdays, except for her coaching call. Instead, she focuses on deep work, like reading, research, or writing.

3. **Brainstorming Thursdays:** Steph reserves Thursdays for hashing out ideas or working within a small group to problem-solve.

4. **TGIF Fridays:** Even in a remote world, it's critical to maintain connections. Steph schedules her social calls for Fridays, whether inside or outside the company. She might grab a coffee if local or schedule a call to casually check in with someone on a different team that she hasn't talked to in a while.

> ### ❓ REFLECTION QUESTIONS
>
> 1. What chronotype are you? How does it impact your work?
>
> 2. What chronotypes are present on your team? How does it impact how you work together?
>
> 3. What is one change you will make based on the RW Energy Tracker insights—on both the individual and team levels?

MANAGING YOUR TIME

The author and poet Annie Dillard once said, "How we spend our days is, of course, how we spend our lives. What we do with this hour, and that one, is what we are doing. A schedule defends from chaos and whim. It is a net for catching days."[4]

As you can imagine, that quote has been shared on countless motivational posters and Pinterest boards (and now this book). Blogger Tim Urban of *Wait but Why* alludes to similar insights, albeit through the use of stick figures and Microsoft Paint drawings. He mused that if the average person sleeps seven to eight hours a night, that leaves us 1,000 minutes per day. He then drew a 10-by-10 grid to represent our daily life in 10-minute intervals.[5]

You might be asking yourself: Didn't they just go on and on about time not being created equal? Well, yes, but both can be true. The world still operates on a 24-hour cycle, but you'll want to shift work based on your energy within those hours. Some hours are better for sleep. Others are better for work or play.

Visualizing your time as blocks on a grid can make time feel more concrete and lead to important questions, like these: Is that one-hour meeting worth six blocks (or more, if during your peak performance hours)? Will answering that Slack message zap four blocks due to context-switching? If so, maybe you should batch your messages and answer later.

With that in mind, how will you and your team use time wisely?

Set Top Priorities

During their call together, Tam found it weirdly refreshing when Sahar reminded her that they might be dead next week. (Spoiler: We're both still alive as of writing this book.) While we don't want to send you down a rabbit hole of existential doubt, this reminder can be helpful from time to time. Think of it as a memento mori.

Understanding how our brains work can help us better optimize our time and be more discerning about what activities we undertake. According to Sahar, our brains are wired to seek instant gratification and quick sources of dopamine. (Hence that gravitational pull toward Instagram and online news.)

Rather than fight against it, Sahar suggests, we can accept it, embrace it, and work with it—by developing systems to get our most important tasks done first and feel good after completing them!

There are a few systems for prioritizing critical activities. At DuckDuckGo, Ali and her team referred to a critical priority as a "Single Top Priority" or their "Critical Path." In Sahar Yousef's productivity lab, they refer to it as "MIT" (Most Important Task). Regardless of terminology, the question remains: What's the one thing you (or your team) need to get done today to feel successful? How can you structure your day so that it gets done?

It can be second nature to revert to your to-do or task list for top priorities, but we encourage you to pause and reflect. What are all the different ways that you could spend your time today? While it feels good to cross actions off your task list (remember that dopamine rush), it might not be the most important. We often forget to include less tangible aspects of work, like strategic thinking or considering ways we could communicate an idea (it's not always a meeting). It's tempting to get so busy doing that we forget the importance of *thinking*.

🔍 SPOTLIGHT STORY: MIT in Practice with Ali Brandt

Ali Brandt, a product manager by trade, lives and breathes prioritizing task lists and product road maps, all from her sunny home office in Berkeley, California. She starts each day by taking stock of everything she needs to do, beginning with her project management system (Asana) in-box. She reviews what's come in from other people, looks at what she's added, and asks herself questions like "What's on my project plan?" and "What's the next milestone?"

After taking stock, she breaks down her tasks into three buckets:

1. **MITs (Most Important Tasks):** This is everything that Ali absolutely *must* get done that day. She tries to limit herself to one or two things and asks herself, "What is the thing that if I get to the end of my day and I haven't accomplished it, I have failed?"

2. **Non-MITs:** Under this second bucket, Ali lists tasks that, *if* she has more time that day, she should get done. These are often smaller tasks that can be bundled together, such as responding to emails or writing up documentation.

3. **Next:** The final bucket focuses on tomorrow (and the days after tomorrow). She lists tasks that she knows will not get done today but will need to happen soon. This helps her create her MITs for the rest of the week.

After spending 15 minutes strategizing her day and breaking tasks into the three buckets, she's ready to start. According to Ali Brandt, "I don't have to think about planning my day after that. This strategy helps me accomplish way more."

That might sound great (in a perfect world), but you may be wondering: What about all those fire drills and inbound messages throughout the day?

According to Ali, "If a Slack message comes in during the day, I table it and immediately create an Asana task, as long as it's not urgent. Rather than get interrupted, I try to batch my Slack and email responses to specific parts of the day." It's all about triage.

This process also applies to thoughts and ideas Ali has throughout the day. "My boss loves that she can give me a complex problem, and I will not drop any balls. I understand all the contingencies because as I think of them, I add them to Asana. I then use my Asana process to incorporate the contingencies into my workflow."

Moving from Inputs to Outputs

Historically, organizations have approached work using a *Field of Dreams* mentality: If you build it, they will come. Leaders have often assumed that if there are butts in seats for at least 40 hours per week, they'll reach the company's goals.

But now, with remote work, we can develop a closer proxy for work than face time. Through documentation, it's easier to show and preserve the outcomes of your work. To move to being an output-oriented team, you can do the following:

🛠 HOW-TO: Manager Checklist for an Outputs-Oriented Team

☐ **Set a "North Star" for your team.** Create a reasonable and achievable goal.

☐ **Break down the North Star goal into digestible chunks.** Divide the goal into concrete tasks, like launching a new product feature or writing a marketing brief.

☐ **Go for quality over quantity.** Don't fall prey to the common trap of conflating the number of things done with actually getting things done. As a manager, focus on measuring the highest-impact activities.

Maker vs. Manager Schedule

When Nick Valluri joined his first fully distributed company, Zapier, he had reservations about remote work. However, he was excited to ditch the three-hour round-trip commute. Within a week, his reservations disappeared: "I was like, wow, where has this been all my life? I'm more productive. I have more ownership of my day and where I allocate my time."

For the first time in Nick's career, he dedicated 80 percent of his time to partnerships. "That freedom to go talk to partners was so liberating. I didn't have to worry about the 10 people I needed to talk to internally and get closure on decisions. That was just happening asynchronously."

Finally, Nick shifted from his manager's schedule (e.g., back-to-back check-in meetings) to a maker's schedule (e.g., working with partners on tech integrations). With Nick's story in mind, let's review ways as a manager that you can get out of the way so that employees can do their best work. (All while maintaining accountability, of course.)

🔧 HOW-TO: Manager Checklist for Balancing a Maker and Manager Schedule

- ☐ **Schedule "you" time:** Have sanctioned days when calendars are purposefully left empty, so that you and your team can get lost in your work. Makers get heads-down time to actually . . . make things. Managers can spend time thinking rather than acting on impulse. If a whole day is hard to plan, block out a few hours or leverage time zone differences to think and tune out.

- ☐ **Check messages in batches:** Checking inbound messages all day is an energy drainer! Encourage your team to batch-respond to messages. Some practical norms might include responding three times per day (morning, lunch, evening) or checking in after completing your MIT.

- ☐ **Communicate expectations:** Culture ultimately is a set of normalized behaviors. As a manager, model the behaviors you desire of your team by over-communicating expectations and setting boundaries on your time. Fight the urge to micromanage, and then get out of the way and let people work!

- ☐ **End meetings swiftly:** Give people their time back if you reach the meeting's objective early. Carlos Silva takes it a step further, opting for "speedy meetings" in Google Calendar, essentially scheduling 25- and 50-minute meetings instead of the standard 30 and 60 minutes.

- ☐ **Record meetings:** Did a teammate miss a meeting because they were deep in work? Ken Weary and Carlos Silva both recommend recording meetings. Ken shares, "This approach gives our team more control of their own time and focus. Plus you can watch at a faster playback speed to save time."

Pro Tip

- Want more direction on how to optimize your calendar? Check out Coda's Color-What-Matters calendar integration and analytics tool, developed by CEO Shishir Mehrotra.[6] Alternatively, Jason Morwick of Cactus Communications recommends downloading your calendar and analyzing your meetings. If it's one-way communication, like updates and reviews, try to move to asynchronous. This foreshadowing advice reflects our RW Meeting Audit, which you'll learn more about in chapter 8.

❓ REFLECTION QUESTIONS

1. Does your team work according to top priorities? If not, how can you create that norm?

2. Are you a maker or a manager, or both? How can you design your schedule to optimize your time?

MANAGING YOUR FOCUS

We've all been there. You know, that meeting that feels like it's happened before. A decision that keeps getting passed around like a hot potato. That reappearing agenda item that makes you want to scream.

Let's call it Groundhog Day for the Americans, a tedious déjà vu for the French, and undoubtedly a circle of hell for the modern remote worker.

As a manager, it's critical to remove blocks and streamline your team's work rather than making it *more* cumbersome.

Streamline Decision-Making

To gain some outside perspective, Tam sat down with Shuhan He, MD, an emergency room physician and instructor at Harvard

Medical School, for Korean bibimbap while he explained his methodology for dealing with life-or-death decisions in the emergency room.

According to Shuhan, when we have a lot of things competing for our attention, it's hard to prioritize. As humans, we often struggle to distinguish the urgent from the important. This usually requires sorting out whether the emergency at hand is life-threatening or not and, from there, creating a decision tree of next steps.

To do this, medical practitioners focus on gathering *salient* information that will enable them to decide if necessary. The rest is all noise, which can confuse rather than clarify. For example, a doctor might rely on a CT scan as salient information to make a go or no-go decision, given that it's a good, reliable, high-fidelity source of information.

How can we apply Shuhan's insight from the ER to remote work? As a manager, you need to decide on a clear decision-making framework for your team so that you can parse the important from the urgent. Once you've decided on the process, gather salient information that will help you make a decision. When possible, clear out the noise and information that's irrelevant to the decision. (Plus, it's a good reminder that your work emergencies are most likely not life-or-death decisions, so keep calm and carry on.)

⚒ HOW-TO: Manager Checklist for Remote Decision-Making

- ☐ **Choose one approach that works for you:** Use off-the-shelf decision-making models for inspiration. We are fans of models such as the 5 Whys, Edward de Bono's PMI model, and the Vroom-Yetton Decision model. Document the process you decide to use in your Digital House for everyone to see.

☐ **Decide the *who* and *how* up front:** Determine who is the final decision maker and the process from the beginning for stakeholder buy-in. Try to eliminate the need for consensus where possible.

☐ **Discuss and evaluate asynchronously first:** Leave space for asynchronous fact gathering and thinking. Include polls, surveys, and diary studies, depending on the level of complexity of the decision to gather objective information. Encourage everyone to provide possible solutions, regardless of location or spot on the introversion-extroversion spectrum.

☐ **Meet only if necessary:** Only meet if a decision cannot be made asynchronously first. If you decide to meet synchronously, make sure that all stakeholders are present and have preread the options and supporting evidence.

☐ **Document all other options and rationale:** Document the decision you moved forward with and the ones you decided to table. This creates an archive of your decision-making history so that colleagues can revisit the logic later on.

☐ **Have an experimental mindset:** Not all decisions need to be final. Try prototyping options if the way forward is unclear. Set a clear time frame and success metrics to compare the options tested.

☐ **Create a decision postmortem:** Communicate the results of the decisions to the people affected and the wider team. Summaries can include a problem statement, the goal, criteria for the decision, alternatives suggested, experiment details (if any), results, and metrics to measure. If it is a contentious decision or a highly sensitive topic, check in with team members afterward.

⌕ SPOTLIGHT STORY: Decision-Making at Zapier

Let's look at how Zapier, an all-remote company, handles decision-making.

Before jumping into the details, Cody Jones, Zapier's global head of partnerships and channels, highlighted the *values* that are needed up front to create a conducive environment for remote decision-making. They included transparency, context, a framework, and discoverability. (Notice any common themes?)

Why are they important? Transparency will ensure that people feel included in key decisions. Context informs people who may be impacted. A framework makes it easy to gather all of the relevant information and sends a signal: a decision will be made. And last, discoverability. As Cody said, "Decisions inevitably live on, sometimes longer than you are in your current role. Ensuring that decisions both are discoverable and have a dedicated home will save you and your teammates tons of hours."

While Zapier's Decision-Making Profiles have evolved, the basics remain the same:

- A high-level summary (e.g., TL;DR)

- What they're trying to accomplish

- Additional background and context

- A few decision options with related trade-offs

- Specific feedback they needed from individuals

According to Cody, it worked, but there was a gap: "The Decision-Making Profile we had early on was a fast, effective way of getting to decisions made. But it didn't clarify which roles everybody should play. Every vote was equal. To a degree, it led to group decision-making that could slow things down."

That was when they introduced DACI to the process:

- **Driver:** Gathers information from the teams and proposes a way forward.

- **Approver:** Gives the stamp of approval (or not).

- **Contributor:** Provides relevant subject-matter expertise to inform the decision.

- **Informed:** Won't be driving or consulted but might be impacted by the decision.

As Cody said, "At the end of the day, the Driver is responsible for guiding the teams to a decision and then makes a recommendation to the Approver for a final decision. Afterward, the Decision-Making Profile becomes an artifact that we can refer to and reference in the future."

Think of it in terms of the Supreme Court and case law. Each decision sets a precedent for future decisions. In Cody's role as the head of partnerships, he often points his team to past decisions as a reference for new partnerships. For example, he may highlight a similar situation with Shopify or show a teammate how they handled something with Google that might work with Facebook.

Cody and his team recently used the DACI and the Decision-Making Profile framework to create a partnerships policy for integrating crypto apps on Zapier. Rather than simply allow the integration, they paused to think through the potential consequences. For example, what if somebody messed up a Zap and automatically transferred something? Or thought they were testing the integration but made a transfer instead?

These questions highlighted a more significant decision that needed to be made: What types of apps should be allowed on Zapier? What kinds of functionality should they have for their users?

Setting Boundaries and Creating Rituals

In order to focus, we also need to create boundaries and rituals, or else we run the risk of work taking over our lives. While commuting is tiresome, it did provide a transition—which is still needed in the remote working world.

Nick Valluri clearly illustrated this contention while pointing to his room showcased on the Zoom screen. His video game console and TV set were two feet away from his workstation. He lamented that it's hard to create boundaries when his key downtime activities, playing games and watching shows, are right next to where he does his hardest work. As Nick aptly put it, "Work is in your house now."

Siobhan McKeown of Human Made believes that one way to create boundaries is to care about something outside of work. She forms a boundary between work and her personal life through a simple ritual: she puts her children to bed and then practices the piano for an hour. "It's a transition where I move from thinking about work to not thinking about anything."

Likewise, Cody Jones of Zapier touched on the need for a social life outside of work and his home. At first, it was fantastic to have lunch with his kids every day, but he found that he had all this pent-up energy to interact with people *after* work. That led him to invest in local communities, activities, and religious groups to fill his social needs. And although he initially thought networking groups were a bit lame, he now learns from others in the industry through the Cloud Software Association or Partnership Leaders.

Once again, these real-life stories align with Sahar Yousef's research. She recommends psychologically detaching from both personal and professional responsibilities regularly.

No, that's not a fancy way of saying to scroll social media or the news. She means going entirely off the grid. Her lab recommends using a 3M framework to avoid burnout:

1. Macro breaks (half- to full-day offline per month)

2. Meso breaks (two to four hours offline every week)

3. Micro breaks (a few minutes, multiple times a day)

🔍 SPOTLIGHT STORY: "One Spot, One Goal" Ritual

Ali Greene, half of the brainpower behind this book, fully embraces the work-from-anywhere aspect of remote work to take regular micro breaks.

She's coined this productivity hack "One Spot, One Goal," where she uses her physical environment as a cue to focus on one thing and then takes a break while changing locations. The fresh air and bike ride act as a natural energy boost to help her reset.

Sometimes this looks like a café crawl—where she'll pop into a buzzing breakfast spot to jump-start her morning and then bike to a cool yet quiet café to focus and write a presentation. She concludes the day at home, where she'll give a webinar or pop onto a Zoom call.

Ali even made this hack work during the COVID-19 pandemic when she jumped from kitchen island to sofa to corner nook in her studio apartment.

❓ REFLECTION QUESTIONS

1. What's one ritual you can try as a "commute" from work to personal life?

2. What's one boundary you can set as a team so that everyone can shut off and recharge?

3. How might your team incorporate the 3M framework (macro, meso, and micro breaks)?

💟 ALI'S ADVICE

I love quick little ways to remember things. When it comes to getting things done, my trick is something I call the 3Ps—Process, Proposals, and Project Templates. These three things can help you fight mental fatigue through standardization.

1. **Process:** Develop a set of instructions for approaching routine tasks and find a way to automate when possible.

2. **Proposals:** Create a proposal outline for team members to evaluate whether an activity is a good use of their time and energy. At DuckDuckGo, we often asked, "Why this, now?"

3. **Project Templates:** I am a big believer in templating everything! You can take a complex process and turn it into an easy-to-fill-out form. Why do the extra work of deciding how to present information when you can simply reuse a template? Plug-and-play for the win!

😊 TAM'S TIPS

I love using a question to explore new possibilities. For example, "How can I curate my week to best meet my work requirements *and* personal needs?"

Then, take the question seriously. It's not a "nice to have" or something to think about once you've completed your to-do list. *How you work is how you live your life.*

Once you have a few ideas, test them out and evaluate them. Think of yourself as a scientist, except the subject matter is you! How can you hack or gamify your life so that it works for you?

For example, maybe you want to test if you are more productive at a particular time of day or in a curated environment. Set up a test using a routine task and take notes. Maybe afternoons working in the park are best for one task, but you prefer mornings on your sofa for another one. The following week, try a mini-experiment. Maybe that's moving one synchronous meeting to asynchronous each week.

You don't need to get it right the first time! It's all about experimenting until you find something that works for *you*.

CHAPTER SEVEN

The Remote Blueprint

 TL;DR

This chapter will guide you through an administrative process to analyze "jobs to be done," specifically focusing on goal setting, prioritization, ownership, and accountability. (We know that sounds especially dry, but we'll make it fun!)

At the end of this chapter, you'll be able to do the following:

✓ Move from an input to output mentality (one of the cornerstones of remote work, as explained in chapter 1) and easily define "done" for yourself and your team by setting measurable goals.

✓ Avoid confusion by creating Task Lists, so that your team knows exactly where to start and what work needs to be completed.

✓ Prevent people from duplicating efforts or critical work not getting done by assigning clear ownership and creating a culture of accountability (don't worry, it's not as scary as it sounds!).

CONSIDER THIS. You're managing a team of marketers at a fashion brand that has a knack for creating witty, on-point Instagram campaigns, website content, and community events that people *actually* want to attend. Your company moved to remote-first about six months ago, and the VP of Marketing now wants your team to promote the new line of super-soft, luxury V-neck T-shirts virtually. Usually, your team hosts catered "drink and design" happy hours and a T-shirt designer speaker series at the showroom locally, but you need to rethink how to do an online-only event with national reach this year.

As you begin, you have an end picture of what success looks like. You want your team to create an engaging virtual party for the boutiques that could buy your T-shirt inventory and expand your market outside of the East Coast of the United States. You hope to create an interactive art gallery for the T-shirt designs and include some special surprises, such as a Zoom magic show, and ship all attendees a cocktail-making kit to enjoy during the event.

In all the excitement and rush leading up to the event (only eight weeks away!), you jump in by delegating tasks. Chloe will build out the website promoting the event. Jamal will invite the community and manage attendees. A couple of weeks later, you realize that key activities are falling through the cracks—the invites still haven't been sent out, the website needs more photos, and the addresses of where to ship the cocktail kits are stored in a few different databases. When confronting your team, you learn that not only have Chloe and Jamal been overextended, but Michelle was out sick for a few days and hasn't been able to support the team.

You realize that you have no idea how much is on your team's plate or where the bottlenecks lie in the process. No wonder your team hasn't reached the vision of success you had in mind.

The challenge for the team was clear, but there wasn't enough "scaffolding" or administrative structure to support you, Jamal, Chloe, and Michelle in the execution and ownership of the event.

Yes, this is a fictional story. But swap that event for launching a new software feature or determining quarterly goals for your team. Is it starting to sound familiar?

We've heard similar stories. This is a challenge that many remote managers face when ensuring alignment to a specific goal, planning the work to be done, and establishing clear ownership and accountability.

🔍 SPOTLIGHT STORY: Falling through the Cracks

Carlos Silva, a remote marketing and content manager, could relate to this fictional story. He explained that at one point in his career, he jumped from working independently at a small start-up to being part of a team collaborating together, after a hiring spree. Knowing that having visibility of the work to be done was necessary for the team's success, Carlos pushed the team to adopt a project management system.

According to Carlos, they used Trello in name only. "No one *really* checked it, and no one tracked that it was being properly used (or not). There was also no documentation on using the tool or how to track projects." As you can imagine, this led to team chaos. People were working on the same projects; others fell through the cracks.

They had focused so much on which tool to use that they'd forgotten the most important part: how they would use it together to accomplish their goals.

Carlos learned the hard way that you need a culture of transparency, a well-structured project management system (or Digital House), and proper documentation of the House Rules to run projects successfully. According to Carlos, House Rules need to be "written clearly, publicly accessible, and within a tool that serves. It's the single source of truth."

THE RW BLUEPRINT EXERCISE:
A FOUR-STEP FRAMEWORK

Imagine how easy planning and project management would have been for Jamal, Chloe, and Michelle if they had taken the lessons learned from Carlos Silva.

We, too, have learned these lessons over time. Early in Ali's career, Ali was part of the team that decided whether specific sales deals were worth the time and effort at LivingSocial. (Yes, this was 2010—remember the group coupon craze?) The Research team spent a lot of time coordinating between Sales and Operations, making one-off decisions, and forgetting agreements after meetings ended.

Ali saw the need to develop a transparent process; hence Project "CRUSH" (because it helped "crush" sales goals) was born. While Ali had the vision for a tool that would suggest sales and operational guidelines based on city metrics (e.g., population, internet-friendliness), it was her first in-depth attempt at creating a company-wide process involving moving pieces. Rather than planning the project up front, Ali just got to work—stopping and asking questions whenever she got stuck—and later needed to get buy-in from the teams while teaching them how to use the tool.

After too many late nights, she decided there had to be a better way to stay organized and proactively get buy-in from stakeholders. Going forward, Ali learned how to identify key people whose knowledge would help the project's success and how to communicate a project plan. Years later, at a different start-up, a coworker nicknamed her "Ms. Process," so we think she succeeded.

While there are lots of project management philosophies and frameworks out there, in this chapter we will walk you through our signature RW Blueprint for you to facilitate with your team. Plus, we'll continue to imagine how things might have unfolded for Jamal, Chloe, and Michelle had they been using this process.

It's a simple, four-step process that can work across situations—from a small project to an intricate multiteam product launch. It can take a few minutes, a few hours, or a few days to complete, based on the level of complexity of the task. It all comes down to goal setting, creating a Task List, determining the top priorities, assigning ownership, and setting accountability norms.

By doing this administrative work at the start, your team will save a lot of time and stress in the future. A good process isn't meant to add more work to your plate. Rather, it's a set of rules that make real work more manageable in the future.

This "cheat sheet" is a reference, both for learning the process in this chapter and for managing your next project (figure 7.1). It might even make some nice furniture in your Digital House as your team builds their project management muscles.

Now that we have a common framework, here is a sneak preview of where Jamal, Chloe, and Michelle are going in their quest to design the coolest online T-shirt launch in history. The result? Their hard work paid off, and they secured inventory in 20 new boutiques in stores in Austin, Texas; Savannah, Georgia; Detroit, Michigan; and even Los Angeles, California!

So while we settle in and bask in their fake success, let's break down each step of the RW Blueprint for you to do with your team (for "guaranteed" real results).

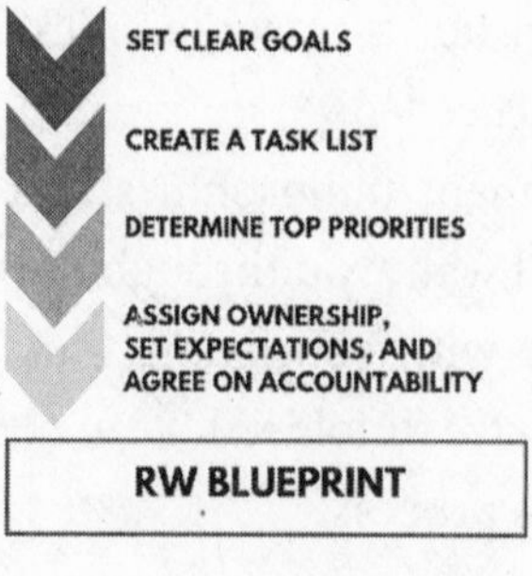

SET CLEAR GOALS	RW BLUEPRINT OUR GOAL: _____				
CREATE A TASK LIST	THEME	TASK	DRI	PRIORITY	CADENCE / MILESTONE EXPECTATIONS
DETERMINE TOP PRIORITIES					
ASSIGN OWNERSHIP, SET EXPECTATIONS, AND AGREE ON ACCOUNTABILITY					
RW BLUEPRINT					

FIGURE 7.1 RW Blueprint Framework

HOW-TO: Set Clear Goals

The first step in completing anything is knowing where you want to go. This exercise is aimed to help you set a clear goal, or end state, for your project.

But it's important not to conflate objectives with completion. Mike McNair aptly compared it to shooting an arrow at a target. "The objective is to hit the target. Completion means I actually hit the target. Between objective and completion, there's a lot of iteration and clarification going on."

As with the RW Team Mission Statement and RW Team Charter exercises, we recommend having your team first reflect independently on a set of questions about goals and aspirations and then come together to flesh out the official goals leading up to the project kickoff.

Here are a few questions that can help crystallize your project-specific goals and objectives:

- How does this project help us accomplish our team's overall mission?
- What do we plan to do?
- What will change if this project or team succeeds?
- What does "done" look like?
- How will we measure success?

After everyone has had a chance to share their perspective first asynchronously, validate and document the final agreed-upon goal. Be as specific as possible. For example, "Selling more shirts" would be too vague for our fictional T-shirt friends. Instead, after they finished the exercise, they decided on the following goal: "To execute a virtual event to launch the new V-neck line on October 19. The launch should be focused on customers outside the Metropolitan DC area, resulting in at least 50 returning plus 50 existing customers in attendance. Success will be measured by secured inventory in new boutiques (at least five new markets) and ROI (at least two times the cost of the event in purchase inventory)."

Pro Tips

- Keep it simple. Focus on one goal at a time. If there are multiple goals that your team wants to cover, we recommend breaking it up into a multipart exercise.
- Goals should be specific, measurable, and actionable. Try to incorporate your existing measurement tools rather than inventing from scratch.

⚒ HOW-TO: Create a Task List

Once you have a goal in mind, it's time to take inventory of what everyone is already working on before you can add new tasks related to the goal. It's human nature to get excited about a new project and want to start working full-steam ahead. But unless you carve out the time to analyze what everyone is *already* doing, it will be challenging to understand your team's previous commitments, which might hinder or distract them from reaching the RW Blueprint Goal.

In order to get a complete picture of what everyone is currently working on (e.g., Business as Usual "tasks") *and* what new activities must be accomplished to reach your RW Blueprint Goal set in step one (e.g., Blueprint "tasks"), we recommend building a Task List. A Task List is the "single source of truth" for what's on the team's plate with all the tasks that need to be completed. It may be in sequential order or based on themes. This process allows you to dig into the nitty-gritty details of the project and uncover unforeseen tasks and interdependencies required to reach the goal.

The team members should create their Task Lists individually, so they can analyze how they are spending their time and how they plan on contributing to the RW Blueprint Goal. We believe there's nothing like getting that anxious "I-have-so-much-to-do" swirl out of your head and onto (digital) paper. Later on, you'll review each other's Task Lists together to see what should be reshuffled among team members.

You'll want every team member (including yourself!) to jot down tasks in two buckets:

1. **Business as Usual Tasks:** All of the routine tasks and existing activities that your team is currently or will be doing that overlap with the RW Blueprint Goal timeline. This may include nonroutine tasks if you are involved in more than one special project. You may look back at your calendar and job description if you have trouble populating this list. Don't try to eliminate yet—that's for a later step!

2. **Blueprint Tasks:** This is a forward-thinking list, where you brainstorm all the necessary steps to accomplish your RW Blueprint Goal. In order to accurately speculate what needs to be done to accomplish the RW Blueprint Goal, you may look at past project plans to forecast what steps should be taken or work backward from your final goal and ask yourself, "What needs to be completed to reach the goal?"

Pro Tips

- Don't constrain yourself. Right now, you should be focused on adding, not deleting. You want to gather a clear picture of the entire universe of things your team is working on.
- Encourage the team to be honest. This is a no-judgment zone.
- For smaller projects, you may choose to skip one of the lists or do this in your head.

Once everyone has finished their Task Lists, synthesize them into a Main Team Task List under these two categories: Business as Usual tasks and Blueprint tasks. You'll bring this with you to step three to set Top Priorities.

This is a great time to see if multiple people are working on the same thing (red flag!) or if no one is accountable for something important (double red flag!). During this step, our fictional T-shirt friend Jamal discovered that the invites still hadn't been sent out. It wasn't on his Task List, but it also wasn't on Chloe's.

🛠 HOW-TO: Determine Top Priorities

Remember how we told you to *not* delete anything from your Main Team Task List yet? Well, now is the time! Let's start prioritizing.

It is easy to want to prioritize in theory, but in practice, it is just as easy to get derailed. Maybe you feel emotionally compelled to help a team member, even though you don't have the time right now. Or, like Chloe, Jamal, and Michelle, you prioritized the urgent pings from your manager—even though they weren't necessarily essential or important.

In chapter 6, we discussed day-to-day strategies to get your work done, like MIT (Most Important Task) and defining a North Star. You can apply these concepts at a macro level during this step. Rather than deciding on a single MIT for your day, you can set a weekly North Star to guide your team in the right direction across the project. If all else fails or goes off the rails on a given day or week, what's the one thing that must happen to keep the project on course? For the project to succeed, what are the three to five MITs that will help you reach your RW Blueprint Goal?

For example, it is critical for Jamal and his team to send the invites. Otherwise, no one will know about the event, but the event could likely still succeed without the presence of the virtual magic tricks.

After determining your RW Blueprint Goals MITs and North Star, we recommend that you revisit your Main Team Task List with a scrutinizing eye. When prioritizing, you need to make tough choices; otherwise, it's merely a laundry list.

We like to use the exercise "Stay, Start, Stop, Shift" to help you prioritize.

- **Stay:** Business as Usual tasks that need to continue during the RW Blueprint project.

- **Start:** Tasks you need to start pronto to accomplish your RW Blueprint goal.

- **Stop:** These are the tasks that take a lot of time *and* are out-of-scope. This might be a bit hard at first, but recognize that stopping activities will give you the time, energy, and focus to prioritize the tasks that really need to be done.

- **Shift:** These are tasks that need some tinkering. You may want to automate them, delegate them to another team member, or outsource them to a contractor.

If struggling to prioritize, you can ask the following questions:

- **For Business as Usual Tasks:** If I stopped doing this task during the course of the Blueprint project, what would happen?

- **For Blueprint Tasks:** Is this required to reach our goal?

Now it's time to cross items off your list, as promised! We recommend removing any Stops from the Main Task List and rethinking any Shifts.

Once you have a prioritized Main Task List, you'll need to differentiate tasks. Which ones need to be started first? Which ones are more time-consuming than others? Do tasks need to be completed in a specific order?

You can use a simple three-point scale, such as low-medium-high, to indicate urgency or a chronological prioritization, like now, near, and far. Whatever scale you use, make sure to define what each label means. For example, is "near" in two weeks or two months?

Our fictional friend Jamal made a few tough decisions about tasks originally on his list during this step. He has stopped his biweekly calls with community partners. This should have been transitioned to the Partnerships team six months ago, and the project is a great forcing function to make the introduction. He also stopped brainstorming for an internal design contest for December. The contest is internal-facing and not a top priority; therefore, it can be postponed. Jamal also decided to shift all of his content marketing tasks, like social media posts and blogs, to promote the October 19 event rather than build out two content streams.

🔍 SPOTLIGHT STORY: How to TIER Priorities

Remember how Ali used to teach those productivity workshops back in the early days of her career? She'd often receive questions from frustrated junior-level employees along the lines of "What if everything is both urgent and important? How should you prioritize?"

Calmly, she always responded, "Well, if everything is urgent and important, then nothing is urgent and important." For times when that flippant statement did not put the question to rest, Ali introduced a TIER (time, impact, effort, and revenue) acronym to help teams judge and prioritize tasks based on objective measures for (yep, you guessed it) TIER-ing your priorities.

1. **Time:** Is there a looming, external-facing deadline? Is the timeline for completing this task a contingency for other parts of the project?

2. **Impact:** What is the impact of a particular task on the success of the project, team, or company?

3. **Effort:** What will be the level of effort required to complete the task? Is it something that can be grouped with other low-effort tasks, or can it be further broken into smaller tasks that can be analyzed with the Stay, Start, Stop, Shift method?

4. **Revenue:** When all else fails, is it a revenue-generating activity (or, for nonprofits, a fundraising activity)? What is the ROI on completing the activity?

By reflecting on those questions, Ali found that teams and managers were able to make clearer and more confident prioritization decisions.

✂ HOW-TO: Assign Ownership, Set Expectations, and Agree on Accountability

Take a deep breath! You're almost done. Now it's time to turn all of this plotting and planning into action, which requires ownership and accountability. It's time to delegate.

First things first: let's make sure we're using common language.

- **Ownership:** An owner, also known as the DRI (directly responsible individual), is the leader and final decision maker for the task or project. The owner is not necessarily the person completing the task single-handedly but rather the person who is accountable for the quality and success of the work.

- **Accountability:** The act of holding a person responsible for meeting expectations and commitments. This can happen through workforce processes, person-to-person check-ins, and progress tracking. (Ideally, without the manager breathing down your employee's virtual back.)

Some tasks will have natural owners, but others might be fuzzier (hence the need for clear ownership). You may also discover through the RW Blueprint process that one person has too much on their plate, while another may have too little. You'll want to reshuffle tasks across owners to ensure an equitable workload split across the team.

As a manager, consider the following when determining DRIs for tasks:

- **Expertise:** Who has the capability or unique ability to get this job done?

- **Excitement:** Who is most excited about the job?

- **Energy:** Who has the bandwidth or energy to complete the task?

Once you've assigned DRIs, we recommend enlisting them to set tangible expectations related to the assigned task. As Siobhan McKeown of Human Made said, "In our culture, freedom relies on accountability. Remote work relies on accountability. If people aren't trying to get the job done and take responsibility for themselves, it just doesn't work."

Setting tangible expectations and accountability norms will ensure that your DRIs can work independently toward a goal. It also gives them more skin in the game to problem-solve through obstacles.

Expectations and accountability should include the following:

- A deadline or cadence (if it's a recurring task)

- Accountability agreements (e.g., do you expect weekly updates?)

- OKRs (objectives and key results) and performance metrics (e.g., what does success look like?)

$\mathcal{P}$ SPOTLIGHT STORY: Directly Responsible Doisters

At Doist they keep track of work, set goals, and hold people account-able using a few principles. According to Andrew Gobran, "Across the whole company, we implemented something that we call DRD, which is Directly Responsible Doister. It is how we create trans-parency around who owns what within each team. . . . Each team [identifies] what the core responsibilities are and who is going to be responsible for them. For example, I am the DRD for all our hiring and recruitment. I'm the point of contact for that."

This concept, while relatively simple in theory, is essential in prac-tice, as it unlocks the ability for companies to operate with a sense of ownership. From there, owners set clear goals of what they are trying to accomplish and report asynchronously on the performance metrics. Chase confirms, "Everybody's empowered to do their work, without question. Everything is kept in transparent places. Every-body is held accountable. Things are reported daily and weekly, all asynchronously. We're able to keep work moving seamlessly without a lot of interference from management."

RW BLUEPRINT IN ACTION

We recommend having a template, like the one shared at the begin-ning of the chapter, that you can reuse with your team and save in your Digital House. If you're using a specific tool for project manage-ment, like Asana or Notion, consider keeping the template accessible in the tool for quick and easy use. Ultimately, your RW Blueprint should be easy to understand and find so that it is usable by your team.

🔍 SPOTLIGHT STORY: RW Blueprint in Action for M&A

Tam couldn't believe her luck. Her company had acquired Tumblr from Verizon, just as her manager left on a planned three-month sabbatical. She was tasked to lead the M&A integration of 200 employees with their own IT systems, HR processes, and policies under a tight timeline. Nervous to execute such a high-profile project alone but excited about the development opportunity, Tam asked a former teammate to delay his transfer to another team. Together, they worked through a plan for Day One readiness. (Thanks again, Patrick.)

They created a Task List by functional area with *all* the tasks required for the M&A integration and then prioritized them. Some tasks needed to be completed on Day One (when Tumblr legally became a part of Automattic), like payroll and specific IT systems. Others could be delayed as long as they were completed in the first 90 days after integration, like moving the Tumblr team to a temporary coworking location while deciding if they'd maintain an office. They then assigned DRIs (directly responsible individuals) for each functional category of the integration, like legal, HR, IT, and PR, which included representatives from Tumblr's leadership team.

Every Monday, Tam and Patrick collected asynchronous task updates from each DRI and then helped unblock any contingencies or hold-ups. The integration went smoothly, which Tam attributes to the clear goals, detailed Task Lists, and awesomely accountable DRIs for each part of the integration. The team accomplished a ton of work quickly, and Tam smiles whenever she reads about Tumblr having a resurgence with Automattic as its parent company—with a new Gen Z cult following. (She's since revived her Tumblr account.)

Now that you've seen the RW Blueprint in action, we recommend trying it with your team. The RW Blueprint is an exercise, process, and tool to make the unknown known and structure chaos. We hope that by having frank and transparent conversations with your team, you can truly understand the task at hand and create a plan to get there. And we hope that by taking the time to structure your work, you can save unnecessary frustration and miscommunication down the road. As Ben Franklin once said, "If you fail to plan, you are planning to fail"!

> **❓ REFLECTION QUESTIONS**
>
> 1. How can you use the RW Blueprint with your team?
> 2. Where does your team naturally excel in the RW Blueprint process (e.g., goal setting, Task Lists, setting top priorities, assigning ownership, and keeping accountability)? Where could they improve?
> 3. How can you adapt this exercise for your individual workflow?

💬 ALI'S ADVICE

Don't get bogged down in the details or the how-to. Eventually, the RW Blueprint can become a simple mental exercise that you run through before kicking off a project instead of going methodically step-by-step, as outlined in this chapter.

For me, this activity has become second nature. Whether I'm working on an independent project or leading teams, I naturally run through the four high-level areas quickly (Goal Setting, Task Lists, Top Priorities, Ownership, and Accountability) in my head to structure work. I have used a remote blueprint to create a project plan for hosting a webinar and facilitated the entire series of exercises as part of an in-depth retreat.

Ultimately, it's all about the larger themes of goal setting, ownership, and accountability. Depending on the goal, the RW Blueprint can be as simple or as complex as needed to bring clarity and organization to your team. Find fun ways to make it your own!

☺ TAM'S TIPS

Do not be afraid to ask questions and challenge the status quo. It is just as important to stop and shift work activities as it is to start them.

Once again, call upon your inner Marie Kondo and find ways to tidy up your work life. Thank projects and tasks that once had meaning, and then politely remove them from your Task List.

Sometimes you need to let go of old work, mental models, and projects to make room for new work and challenges.

CHAPTER EIGHT

ABC of Remote Communication

 TL;DR

In this chapter, we'll cover the key elements of communication and share our mindset for effective remote communication, "Asynchronous Before Calls." You'll learn how to discern when to use asynchronous (later) versus synchronous (real-time) communication and improve your messaging for clarity and actionability.

Disclaimer: This chapter gets pretty granular. Effective and efficient communication unlocks the ability of your team to incorporate *all* of the advice shared throughout this book. However, if you get lazy in your communication, things can unravel quickly.

At the end of this chapter, you'll be able to do the following:

✓ Get really good at asynchronous communication. This is simply a nonnegotiable.

✓ Save your team (and yourself) from too many unnecessary meetings. Reduce Zoom fatigue and make meetings worth the time. (Your CFO will thank us!) When you do meet, make it meaningful and fun!

✓ Prevent conflict by recognizing misunderstandings in communication. Learn how to operate under the principle of "Most Respectful Interpretation."

✓ Be inclusive! Utilize the power of various communication methodologies and tools to flex to the different needs of your team.

✓ Unleash the potential of remote work by writing transparent, concise, and clear messages. Your team will no longer need "just a quick second" of your time to clarify points or unblock a bottleneck issue. They can work seamlessly without ping-pong, back-and-forth communication.

WHEN SARA ROBERTSON first entered the workforce, it looked very different from the world she operates in today. She left Scotland for the States for a summer during university to sell children's books door-to-door. It was early in the advent of mobile phones, and UK mobile phones simply didn't work in the US. The technology was different.

Since her team couldn't easily call or text each other, there had to be a clear plan in place and check-in points with voicemail-box systems. Sara would go to a pay phone (remember those?), dial a number, and receive or leave messages. "There was a rhythm to it. You would check in, and everybody would know the plan and objectives. You could go a whole day or a whole week without really talking to each other."

Sara noticed that when mobile phones worked, the group lost their ability to organize themselves. "It was because we could communicate all the time that we became less organized and less thoughtful." The always-on, always-there technology we have now enables people to do things without thinking. And as Sara said, "Remote work requires a lot of thought. The lack of limits prevents us from making good decisions."

With all our various forms of communication—from phone calls to Zoom, email to WhatsApp, Instagram snaps, TikTok, and LinkedIn—there's an assumption that more communication *must* be better. Right? Or why would we be frantically checking our phones all the time?

But what if more communication isn't necessarily *better* communication?

THE ELEMENTS OF COMMUNICATION

Think about some of the messages you have received in the past week. The news articles you scrolled through while waiting in the grocery line, the photos you liked on Instagram, the conversation you had with a classmate while waiting for yoga to start. Maybe you laughed at a joke and then sent a cry-laugh emoji. Or you sat through a webinar and a calendar notification popped up for your next meeting.

These may all seem different, but ultimately they all share common elements. Let's unpack them.

The Communicators: Individuals, Groups, and Systems

Regardless of the medium, there are essentially three types of communicators—*individuals*, *groups*, and *systems*—who can send or receive messages.

You may type an update into a project management tool (individual → system), and then the next morning you might receive an automated compiled update to you (system → individual).

Or you may have a one-on-one chat with your manager (individual → individual) or receive an announcement on a benefits change from your HR team (group → group). Or maybe you gave a presentation to your key stakeholders (individual → group).

Interactions: One-Way, Two-Way, Project-Based

Now that you've thought about *who* is sending and receiving the message, it's time to reflect on the intended *interaction*.

One-Way Communication

One-way communication is where one communicator shares information with a person, group, or system that does not need further discussion—for example, alerts, project status updates, or vacation announcements.

Two-Way Communication

Two-way communication is where information is being reacted to by one or more communicators, each sharing new perspectives or information. This might be a Q&A session on a new policy or providing feedback on a deliverable.

Project-Based Communication

While both one-way and two-way communication can happen in project management, communication about a project can be more robust and therefore deserves its own mini-category. In this type of communication, it is helpful to think about all communication tied to getting the work done—such as project planning and prework for meetings and brainstorming sessions.

Transparency: Explicit vs. Implicit

Within communication, there will be elements that are *explicit* and *implicit*.

Explicit Communication

The core of the message is stated clearly, leaving no room for doubt or misinterpretation.

Implicit Communication

It's the opposite of explicit. It's the negative space. The message is often implied or assumed. It might include reading between the lines or picking up on body language.

As Andrew Gobran of Doist put it, "Explicit is easier to define. It is what you see in front of you. You hear it, and you read it. It's stated clearly, leaving no room for doubt or misinterpretation. Implicit is the nonverbal, nonwritten aspects. It can be your tone, body language, all of those things. It's fascinating to think about in the context of remote work because implicit communication is very nuanced and difficult to pull off when you lean toward a more asynchronous written format."

Timing: Synchronous vs. Asynchronous

Synchronous Communication

Synchronous communication happens in real time. Not limited to face-to-face interactions, synchronous communication can also include Zoom, back-and-forth convos on Slack, email tag, or phone calls.

Asynchronous Communication

Asynchronous communication is slower by design. It is communication where two or more communicators are not participating simultaneously. The responder is empowered to communicate later. While the tools may look the same, like email or Slack, the expectations are different. The recipient can respond when it's convenient.

The difference between these two definitions can be summarized in two words: *now* and *later*.

For ages, these concepts have been around, from carrier pigeons to letters (asynchronous) to town hall meetings (synchronous). As long as we have had communication, we have created ways to share information both now and later. However, because advancements in technology have changed the work landscape, we now have even more choices in the tools we use to communicate—making the means just as critical as the message.

✎ EXERCISE: Putting It Together

We just threw a lot at you. Let's put it into practice.

1. Choose two types of communication you received recently: one clarifying, one confusing.

2. Imagine the scenario: What happened? Where did the communication happen? What was the message?

3. Reflect and identify the following (table 8.1):

TABLE 8.1 Elements of Communication

THE ELEMENTS	THE TYPES	IDENTIFY
Communicators	Individual, groups, or systems	Who gave and received the communication?
Interaction	One-way, two-way, or project-based	What type of response did you expect? What happened in reality?
Transparency	Explicit vs. implicit	What parts of the message were explicitly stated? What was implicit?
Timing	Synchronous vs. asynchronous	Was the response expected now or later? How long was your attention captured?

4. Think about its effectiveness: What went well? What was frustrating? How could the elements have been changed to make it more effective?

UNLOCKING THE ABC OF REMOTE COMMUNICATION

Of all the elements of communication discussed, there's one aspect that can truly unlock the power of remote work: synchronous versus asynchronous communication. This is the cornerstone of remote work that we call the "ABC of remote communication," an acronym to remember: asynchronous before calls.

This shift requires behavioral changes in individuals and teams. It is more nuanced than having great written communication skills (though that helps!). It's about knowing when, how, and why this all matters.

Better communication with fewer meetings sounds like a dream come true, right? First, let's take a real-time assessment of where your communication stands today.

✎ EXERCISE: RW Team Communication Assessment

Reflect on your current types of communication (one-way, two-way, and project-based) and determine whether you're primarily using async or sync communication today. (Remember, back-and-forth emails are still sync if you're expected to respond now, not later!)

Then rate the effectiveness and reflect on *why* (table 8.2). At the end of the chapter, we'll help you make changes for the better moving forward.

TABLE 8.2 RW Team Communication Assessment—First Take

COMMUNICATION EVENT	PRIMARY FORMAT (CIRCLE ONE)	RATE EFFECTIVENESS (1 = ☹; 5 = ☺)	REFLECTIONS (WHY WAS THIS FORMAT CHOSEN?)
One-way communication			
Team announcements	Async // Sync		
Personal updates	Async // Sync		
Status updates	Async // Sync		

(continued)

TABLE 8.2 RW Team Communication Assessment—First Take *(continued)*

Two-way communication			
Brainstorming and collaboration	Async // Sync		
Ad-hoc questions	Async // Sync		
Relationship building	Async // Sync		
Conflict resolution	Async // Sync		
Performance feedback	Async // Sync		
Project-based communication			
Project coordination and planning	Async // Sync		
Project kickoffs	Async // Sync		
Project feedback and iteration	Async // Sync		
Add Your Own . . .			
. . . .	Async // Sync		
. . . .	Async // Sync		

Views from the Field: To Sync or Async, That's the Question

Let's take a look at a few experts' opinions on when they opt for each format.

When to Go Asynchronous . . .

Planning and Coordination

"Asana is about coordination. What are we going to do? When are we going to do it? You have clarity on what needs to happen.
. . . If you're spending meetings on that, that's a waste of time."

—ALI BRANDT, PRODUCT LEADER

"Asynchronous is helpful for laying out a plan and milestones. Those things take time to digest. They can't understand it in a purely auditory form." —STEPH YIU, WORDPRESS VIP

Getting Things Done

"People are free to work on their own time and then come together for collaboration, frequently, but in small bursts."
—JACLYN RICE NELSON, TRIBE AI

"We never have scheduled calls on Wednesdays unless it is an emergency. . . . We do this to protect our team from the calendar creep of meetings and optimize a state of flow." —KEN WEARY, HOTJAR

Thinking, Reflecting, and Reasoning

"By default, written text is your friend. Unlike on a call, it gives each person time to think about something before responding. Async can also be spoken audio or a video using Loom or Yac, or even Slack. You can drop a video recording. It's so powerful, especially when people are working in different time zones. You're not interrupting whatever they're doing. They can answer you asynchronously later."
—PHIL FREO, CLOSE.COM

"Collaboration can also happen asynchronously. I think sometimes you need to let ideas sink into your mind. We often see our best ideas come when you're taking a shower or a walk in nature. That is still a collaboration because maybe you've been inspired by a conversation or something you read. And then when you're walking somewhere, all of a sudden those ideas merge." —LAÏLA VON ALVENSLEBEN, MURAL

When to Go Synchronous . . .

Brainstorming, Iterating, and Clarifying

"And then there's the brainstorming, the iteration, the stuff where you don't have clarity on, like, what are we actually going to be doing. There's value in having a conversation because if you tried to do that over Slack, it would be 50 messages, and you wouldn't get anywhere. It's really thinking about what needs to be synchronous versus asynchronous." —ALI BRANDT, PRODUCT LEADER

Building Momentum and Celebrating

"When you really want to celebrate or get visibility, you've got to take it to the weekly team call. . . . Let's say you want to celebrate a customer story, or a new feature launch, or something that the team doesn't think about day-to-day. That needs to be synchronous. People feel excitement around the squishy, untouchable feeling of things."
—STEPH YIU, WORDPRESS VIP

Relationship Building and Resolving Conflict

"There are a few cases where synchronous communication is really good: one-on-ones, relationship building, anytime there's more of an emotional or sensitive topic, like when people are upset about something or are getting frustrated, or if asynchronous back-and-forth discussion is just taking too long." —PHIL FREO, CLOSE.COM

ASYNCHRONOUS COMMUNICATION: DEEP DIVE

Written communication is the backbone of all asynchronous communication. It is searchable, it's formattable, and it can easily be consumed *later* (after storing in your Digital House!). But with the growth of remote work, the medium has expanded: from audio notes to videos and even collaborative whiteboards.

The benefits stay the same regardless of the tool or the medium of asynchronous communication you choose—audio, picture, video, or a combination thereof.

Asynchronous communication does the following:

- Allows for deep focus and fewer interruptions

- Provides time to think, prepare, and produce a response

- Makes room for different time zones and communication styles

- Allows for documentation as default, which increases transparency

The Only Asynchronous Lesson You Will Ever Need (OALYWEN)

We know this is a bold statement (hence we came up with an even more ridiculous acronym to accompany it), but we believe this is the one and only lesson you need to remember when it comes to asynchronous communication, completely agnostic of any fancy tool you wish to use.

OALYWEN is simple, really.

First, you set your expectations, using the 4Ws listed—clarify the following:

1. **Who** is directly responsible for communicating back and what the role of the others on the team should be (e.g., are they solely listeners, or can they chime in?).

2. **What** the deliverable looks like for both the DRI and the others and how it will be used.

3. **When** a response is needed for all involved. Be specific. It is not enough to say ASAP or end of the day, as these things vary from person to person. Use time zones for all involved.

4. **Wah-Wah**—what will happen if there is no response, and what the next steps will be.[1]

Then structure your workflow:

1. **Choose** the tool to be used and how people should respond. For example, if in Slack, should you use threads? If in Asana, should it be a comment or a subtask?

2. **Share** the background/context of your request.

3. **Explain** the content/assignment of the communication.

Let's put OALYWEN into practice using a fictional story.

✎ EXERCISE: Kayaks and Miscommunication

The situation: Levi is the CEO of Kawana Kayaks (loosely inspired by Ali's time coliving in Montenegro). In addition to managing his on-site tour guides, he oversees a remote team of web designers, content creators, and salespeople. They are collaborating on the first redesign of the website (after completing the Blueprint, of course!).

The players: Rue, based in Spain, is on point as the directly responsible individual (DRI). Joe and Abhi, based in Ohio and London, respectively, are collaborating on the redesign.

The communication: Levi has two questions for the team based on Rue's latest user experience study. Due to the time difference and his upcoming holidays, Levi hopes to resolve most of this before the team meeting on Friday; it is currently Wednesday.

Even though their House Rules call for project updates in Asana and Slack for casual conversation, Levi is in a rush. He shoots off a Slack message in the #TeamRemote Slack channel.

Immediately after Levi hits "send," he realizes his mistake. Not only did he break a House Rule, but he forgot the most critical aspects of asynchronous communication! So what should Levi do?

Let's compare his first message and what he did after remembering the OALYWEN (table 8.3).

TABLE 8.3 OALYWEN Before and After

Levi's first message (written in Slack)
Hey team! Saw the results of the UX Study—have a lot of questions . . . Were the people in the control group in our new target audience or representing our old demographics? How does this impact the feedback we are giving the design team? Please clarify the changes for the mock-ups ASAP today so we can get that over before our team meeting.

Levi's improved message (written in Asana)
Hello Rue and team,
I wanted to follow up on the progress report for the website booking system UX results shared last Friday, May 6. I have two questions about the experiment results you shared?
@Rue two questions:
1. How was the control group selected with our new target audience in mind?
2. How do these new results change the feedback we gave to the design team last Thursday, May 5?
If you could respond with that information on this thread by tomorrow (Thursday, May 12) at 9 a.m. ET / 2 p.m. CEST, we can move forward on looping in the design team for final mock-ups ahead of our team meeting.
@Abhi @Joe—Adding in for transparency, if you have anything to add, please do so in this thread by tomorrow (Thursday, May 12) at 9 a.m. ET / 2 p.m. CEST; if you do not respond, I will assume there are no concerns on your end, in moving forward.
Thanks all!

Looking at the two messages, the new message (applying OALY-WEN) is clearer than his original Slack post, but it might be less obvious *why*. To recap, we recommend checking for understanding using the steps below.

1. Place a heart next to the *who* that is directly responsible for communicating back. Place a star next to the roles of the others on the team.

2. Underline *what* the deliverable looks like for both the DRI and the others.

3. Place a square around *when* a response is needed for all involved.

4. Place a dotted line around the *wah-wah*.

5. Circle the background/context of your request.

6. Double-underline the content/assignment of the communication.

7. Fill in the blank: Asana was a better place to communicate over Slack because _____

_____.

Most Respectful Interpretation

Before we wrap up our section on asynchronous communication, we want to shed light on the dark side of asynchronous communication—when it goes awry. Let's go back to Levi and imagine if he had not resent the messaging applying OALYWEN.

It all started with Levi's original message. Like dominos, it set off a quick set of knee-jerk reactions, leading to confusion and stress across the team. The instinct to defend yourself or resolve issues quickly may seem efficient and good-natured, but it can hurt the team in the long run. Asynchronous best practices, such as documentation and giving time for stakeholders to respond, are just as, if not more, important in these heated moments.

We already know what Levi could have done differently. But when mistakes are made (and they will be—we are all human, after all), the best way to respond is to adopt the mental model of Most Respectful Interpretation (MRI). Ali learned this while at DuckDuckGo from her career adviser and the CEO of DuckDuckGo, Gabriel Weinberg, who also highlighted this concept in his book *Super Thinking*.

MRI is the mental process of assuming the best instead of the worst intentions. Throughout her time at DuckDuckGo, Ali repeatedly leaned on this mental model when potential conflicts crept into communication. In talking with our experts, they also brought up this philosophy and suggested a few best practices.

Establish a Tone of Voice

"You have to be very intentional about your written communication to avoid conveying an unintended tone. Part of this comes with writing style and then using other embellishments like emojis and gifs to help reinforce the tone you're going for. On the flip side, it's also important to realize that you are susceptible to misinterpretation when reading someone's message. Your assumptions about their tone or even just the text itself can lead to frustration where none was intended in the first place. It helps to assume good intent and then seek clarification to understand the person's intent and emotional state."
—ANDREW GOBRAN, DOIST

Be Emphatic to Your Audience

"If you're going to be inconveniencing someone, tell the audience, so they know you empathize with them. If you're making a change to something that affects them, don't just tell them the change. Explain why you're making the change. If the announcement involves a mistake you made, it's generally a good idea to apologize." **—KEN WEARY, HOTJAR**

Ask and Check for Understanding

"You have less context in most interactions. It's very easy to have misunderstandings. One of the values I have is assuming the best intentions. Assume it's a misunderstanding, or at least transparently ask them, 'OK, you mentioned this. I tried to interpret it in the best possible way, but maybe there's something I missed.' Because otherwise, conflicts are amplified." **—MARIO GIULIO BERTORELLI, ATIUM.APP**

Respect Cultural Norms

"We have a value of: act with kindness. I think that involves stepping back and understanding that the way someone writes something might come across as really blunt, but it might be the way they would normally communicate in their language. We have so many employees who don't have English as their first language. Their grasp of English is different, and they don't have the same nuances as you."

—SIOBHAN MCKEOWN, HUMAN MADE

Be Inclusive

"Most neurodivergent employees cannot read between the lines or assume what is expected of them.... [We] struggle with nonverbal communication, can miss social cues, and avoid eye contact like the plague.... I'm often told not to take things too literally. If you say something indirectly, I don't get it all the time."

—CAT CONTILLO, HUNTRESS

🔍 SPOTLIGHT STORY: Yeah, Yeah, Yeahs

Although Julie Armendariz worked for a company that had "assume positive intent" as one of its values, it took experiencing it firsthand for the benefit of the value to truly sink in.

Julie had accepted her first people manager role at a small tech firm and was excited to report to the chief HR officer (CHRO) for the first time in her career. Julie knew she could learn a lot from her *fast*. But there was one catch: Julie didn't know her yet, nor her communication or working styles.

Julie generally operates from a "Try to manage no surprises" mentality. Therefore, during the first few months in her new role, she'd go to the CHRO with a situation and then propose an approach or bring a few solutions to the table. But something caught Julie off-guard . . .

The CHRO's response was often "Yeah, yeah, yeah." Julie had no idea what that meant. She asked herself, did she mean, "Hurry up and get to the point"? Or "You're bothering me with this minutiae. I'm busy!" Or even "I don't care what you do. Do whatever you want."

Underlying all of Julie's interpretations was a theme: fear and negativity. She worried that the CHRO didn't care or wasn't interested in her or her work. Finally, Julie couldn't take it anymore. Three months into the "Yeah, yeah, yeahs," she asked the CHRO what it meant.

Though a bit stunned by her question, the CHRO quickly explained that the "yeahs" were a good thing. It meant that she trusted Julie to proceed with her plan. Of course, Julie was relieved but wished she'd asked sooner. It would have saved three months of stress and worry—all over three words.

Practical Tips

Now that you've got the fundamentals down with OALYWEN and MRI, you can take your asynchronous communication to the next level with some of these best practices.

Formatting and Readability

- Use bullet points, headlines, emojis, and other visual cues for readability.

- Consider the audience and tailor accordingly. Types of tailoring include the length of the message, use of graphics, and format (text, audio, video).

- Recap using the TL;DR methodology (Too Long; Didn't Read). This gives the reader a choice: read the summary or the entire message.

Routines and Response Rates

- Leave an asynchronous footprint even after synchronous communication—such as a meeting recap, action item, or decision summary.

- Standardize asynchronous check-ins to reduce the mental overhead. (Remember Ali's 3Ps: Process, Proposals, and Project Templates.)

- Predefine communication cadences and deadlines with your team (e.g., respond in 24 hours; post your weekly update by 5 p.m. Eastern time).

Accountability and Interactivity

- Ask your team to respond to the message with an emoji to acknowledge receipt of the message or to vote on or react to the content (e.g., "thumbs up" = no questions; "confused smiley" = will add to the agenda of our next team meeting to discuss).

- Include communication norms and expectations in your Team Charter.

❓ REFLECTION QUESTIONS

1. What is one *synchronous* communication you could experiment with making *asynchronous*?

2. What aspect of asynchronous communication is the most challenging for you and your team? What's one thing that could help?

3. When were you last triggered by an asynchronous conversation? How would a Most Respectful Interpretation (MRI) have helped?

SYNCHRONOUS COMMUNICATION: DEEP DIVE

Let's not forget the second part of our remote communication ABCs: the asynchronous before calls. Synchronous communication is still important, especially for building trust, developing relationships, professional growth, and discussing complex content about the work itself.

The True Cost of a Meeting

When we spoke to Jaclyn Rice Nelson, the cofounder of Tribe AI, she told us that she tries to avoid creating incentives where meetings are the only way for people to show their work. It requires a balance, though, since they work with external clients. "If they don't understand it, then you fail. You might as well not have done all that beautiful engineering work."

Therefore, Jaclyn always asks herself, "How can we be conscious of our own time but also use everyone else's time in efficient, effective ways?"

While it may be hard to determine the ROI of building trust, you can convert a meeting into a price tag in dollars, euros, pesos, etcetera (you get the idea). There are a few meeting cost calculators available online, or you can do the math yourself on the Meeting Calculator below:

This back-of-the-envelope calculation is a gut check. Is the juice *really* worth the squeeze? Still, it doesn't account for the time to prepare, context-switching, and the time to wrap up the meeting

---

MEETING CALCULATOR

[Length of meeting] × [Hourly salary per attendee] =
Cost per attendee for meeting

Sum [Cost of *each* attendee] = Total cost of meeting

(including documenting decisions and clarifying action items), nor the opportunity cost. What else could the attendees have been doing with that time?

As mentioned by our ABCs, we believe that remote works best when you move as much communication as possible to asynchronous. However, this might seem impossible if your calendar is packed with back-to-back meetings.

As Ben Brooks, the founder of PILOT, highlighted:

A big unlock is if everyone has one or two fewer meetings a day. . . . We act like meetings are productive, but most meetings are of minimal value. It's a real bug in the system. We are all like, "Let's have a meeting. Let's have a meeting!" assuming that the work will get done. We don't have established ways of actually getting work done outside of meetings. So, instead, we "manage by meetings," which is a massive bug. And extra painful in a remote context.

A meeting audit can guide you toward that big unlock. As Ali Brandt, a product manager, stated, "If your company is having a lot of meetings, you need to look at the meetings you're having. What is the purpose of these meetings? Can we meet that purpose in other ways? Usually, it's happening because people are scared about being out of the loop or leaving someone else out of the loop. Or you're just missing some other key component, like a tool (like Slack or Asana), or strategic alignment to ensure everyone is on the same page."

✎ EXERCISE: RW Meeting Audit

The RW Meeting Audit is a diary study to help you evaluate all of the meetings on your calendar (one-on-ones, phone calls, Zoom team meetings—we mean it all) and seek out areas for improvement. This is an activity you can do individually or as a team. The exercise takes a few hours asynchronously, though you may decide to meet afterward to brainstorm alternatives to group meetings.

First, record. Take a look back at all the meetings you and your team have had on your calendar for at least the past two weeks (though we recommend a month to get a true snapshot). Record in a spreadsheet the background detail for each meeting:

- Is the meeting recurring or ad hoc?

- Who is attending?

- What is the purpose?

- Was there a clear agenda?

Next, reflect. For each meeting, reflect on the following questions and mark notes in the spreadsheet:

- Could this meeting be asynchronous instead?

- Could this meeting be changed in cadence, length, or who attends?

- What meetings do we want to keep, and how can we make them more valuable?

Experiment with the changes. This is your chance to cancel meetings, reschedule to a less frequent cadence, or move to asynchronous communication. A few months later, check in and see how the experiments are working. This activity can be done repeatedly, especially after you sense "meeting creep" taking over your calendar once again.

🔎 SPOTLIGHT STORY: Reclaiming Your Time

It can feel daunting to try to change behavior and norms within a company that already has a set way of operation, especially if it's a meeting-oriented culture. When Tam worked at Google Singapore, she was essentially the last stop for approving $1 billion–plus of annual display and video advertising deals across the Asia Pacific region with the likes of Unilever and GroupM.

As you can imagine, this made her quite popular with the Google sales team. Soon, she found back-to-back meetings on her calendar and Cheshire-cat-smiling account managers popping up behind her desk. Although a part of her ego appreciated the fanfare (it's nice to feel like you wield a bit of power in a large organization), her inner child wanted her time back.

That was when she did her meeting audit and implemented her own House Rule: she would agree to a meeting only if they couldn't hash out the details in a short email exchange.

This freed her calendar. Plus, she had written documentation with *all* the deal context, making it easier to evaluate for approval. It was a play out of her dad's playbook ("Tamara, always get it in writing") and now a play in this book!

It can sometimes be hard to see your calendar through an objective lens. That's when leaning on someone else to help audit your calendar can come in handy. As the head of remote-first, Jason Morwick helps leaders get to the root of the endless meetings (often inertia or fear).

When he challenges leaders on weekly one-on-ones with direct reports, they'll initially claim it's for employee engagement. But then Jason digs deeper: "Are you coaching, mentoring, and providing performance feedback in your one-on-ones? If so, I agree. You should do that synchronously, preferably face-to-face or over video. But if most one-on-ones turn into an update about what you're working on, why do you need a meeting for that?"

Likewise, sometimes Jason's questions will surface unrealized fears. For example, one leader was afraid her team wouldn't read her emails, so she set up meetings instead. Once this was uncovered, they could talk tactically about communication channels and email overload and build simple House Rules, like what Tam implemented at Google.

Whether behaviors are due to fear or to inertia, changing them can be tough. Having an objective measure like the RW Meeting Audit can help you proactively question meeting norms and reclaim your time.

MAKING THE MOST OF MEETINGS

For the meetings that stay on your calendar, you'll want to up your virtual meeting game—so that you communicate authentically, engagingly, and effectively.

You are probably familiar with the basics (there are lots of listicles out there). Still, it's important to establish a strong synchronous communication foundation, so you know when it makes sense to break the rules.

Agenda and Expectations

If it's worth having a meeting, then it's also worth having an agenda and setting expectations for that meeting, preferably asynchronously, so you can give everyone time to reflect and mentally prepare ahead of time. Plus, attendees can add to the agenda, and it provides a "forcing function" to corral the side conversations.

You can also use it to get buy-in. Our coauthor Ali does this by reminding people of the agenda and asking, "What is the one thing you hope to get out of our meeting today?"

Remember the 4Ws for setting asynchronous expectations (Who, What, When, Wah-Wah) as a part of the OALYWEN. You'll want to apply the same concept to meeting behaviors.

- **Who** is the DRI (or facilitator) of the meeting? Will other roles be assigned (note taker, secondary speakers)? Who must attend, and who is optional?

- **What** will be discussed (the agenda), including any prereads?

- **When** will the meeting be scheduled, taking into account time zones? (As an attendee, you should be mindful of *where* you take a call. Is a public space like a café appropriate if you'll be discussing confidential information? Will your kids or pets popping in be welcomed or unwanted?)

- **Wah-Wah:** What happens if you do not attend and how to move forward accordingly.

🔍 SPOTLIGHT STORY: One Person, One Square

When Ali first joined DuckDuckGo, she lived an hour away from a small office that a few employees, including the CEO, used. While the company was fully distributed, this space acted as its headquarters, and employees worldwide were welcome to cowork there.

Ali noticed a surprising behavior; at least, she thought so at the time. Even if several of the meeting attendees were in the office together, they still reverted to their laptops and Zoom log-ins for the meeting, which differed from her past experiences where teams would gather in a conference room and dial-in the remote employees.

When she asked about this strange behavior, a coworker explained the rationale. It's an actionable way to promote a remote-first mentality and inclusivity. Regardless of whether you're dialing in from an office or home, you're given an equal playing field on the Zoom screen. It prevents side conversations from happening in person while on mute and the HQ-versus-remote hierarchy.

Zoom, Zoom, Zoom

These days, synchronous meetings are synonymous with video calls. While video- and audio-conferencing tools such as Zoom, Microsoft Teams, Whereby, and Google Meet have led this movement, there's a psychology behind the technology.

In psychology, the "mere exposure effect" describes how a person may like and therefore build trust for a person or thing merely by being exposed to them. That could look like seeing a familiar cashier at your local bodega or trusting brands you're more familiar with when shopping in the grocery store aisles. Likewise, in remote work, a camera-on approach to video calls can tap into the mere exposure effect. It creates a level of warmth that helps develop connections and build relationships faster than without it.

However, more video calls mean more time staring at a screen (and yourself), leading to eyestrain and "Zoom fatigue." On video calls, attendees choose between Gallery view (which can be over-whelming with too many stimuli) or Speaker view (which helps with focus but fails to give you the same visual cues, such as fidgeting or people spacing out).[2]

Sally Thornton of Forshay Consulting goes against the grain, straying from the Zoom default. "I think there should be just as many walks-and-talks as there are meetings behind a screen. Plus, you don't have to look at yourself, which is exhausting. . . . Audio allows everybody to move. No one has to worry about what they look like."

Similarly, Steph Yiu prefers to have one-on-ones by voice only. "It's more intimate. It allows us to step away from the desk, just like you would get coffee with your boss."

Therefore, weigh the pros and cons of video calls and consider other methods, such as audio-only calls and walking meetings (table 8.4).

TABLE 8.4 Video vs. Audio Calls

CONSIDER USING VIDEO CALLS WHEN . . .	CONSIDER USING AUDIO-ONLY CALLS WHEN . . .
• You are working with a new team and trying to build trust. • You want more emotional or tonal cues. • Everyone agrees and is happy to be on camera. • You want to use interactive features, like chat or visual whiteboard.	• Your internet connection is terrible. • You are in transit. • You have a high degree of trust and can benefit from a screen break. • You are feeling self-conscious. • There are no visuals to share. • You're connecting one-on-one and voice-only feels more personal.

What's in a Background?

Who knew that camera on or camera off had so many layers? Now, let's peel the onion once again. What are you showing to your team if you've opted for camera on? Is the focus on you or your unmade bed in the background? What is the most appropriate (we hate the word *professional*, but frankly it is work) background for your home office? Let's explore.

Clean and Crisp

Think crisp white walls or hip exposed brick. It focuses the eye on you, not what's behind you. This can be a great option if you're leading the meeting and want to avoid distractions.

Unique and Personalized

If you are comfortable, try inviting colleagues into your home virtually. Showing off your space can be an opportunity to build relationships and find surprising ways to connect. For example, Ali once kicked off a meeting with a new employee by asking about the bookshelf behind him, lined with action figures. They quickly bonded over their shared interest in superheroes and Marvel movies. That visual cue sparked a quirky connection.

Virtual Backgrounds

Virtual backgrounds can be polarizing. Some people love virtually dropping into a tropical island or shooting into outer space. It also helps hide the messy bed behind you. Others may find it distracting and lacking authenticity.

As a manager, you may want to create a norm across your team or for specific meetings—especially if there are strong, differing opinions. For example, you may decide to use a virtual background for a team-building meeting with a theme, like visiting your bucket-list locales. Background images of the Galápagos Islands or the Grand Canyon can spur conversation, but maybe you go back to something less distracting when discussing your OKRs for the next quarter.

For employees anxious about showing their space, remember you can always use the blur feature for the best of both worlds!

Five Hacks for Great Video Meetings

Did you know that the mind wanders 30 percent of the time?[3] Therefore, we forgive you if you were just daydreaming—it happens. But how can you design meetings around our haphazard attention spans?

If you ask Vinh Giang, motivational speaker and magician, it all boils down to *vocals*.[4] Our remote experts say the key is in facial expressions, noticing if people are double-tasking, zoning out, or present to the conversation. Our "Five Hacks" are inspired by these people.

You can use these Five Hacks for great video meetings—to be more charismatic and engaging and help your team do the same. Also, it's important to note that you might already have a "hero hack"—something that you excel at IRL (in real life), whether that's making eye contact, active listening, or storytelling. Play to your strengths where possible.

1. Speed

Vary the rate of your speech to maintain interest and signal importance. Slow down for the important bits, and speed up for the parts
you can gloss over. For example, if you're summarizing a preread
at the beginning of the meeting, you can speed up, assuming that
everyone had time to read in depth asynchronously before the call.

2. Melody and Tone

Melody makes points memorable through the arrangement of
sounds. It's why it's easier to remember songs over written blog
posts. You can incorporate melody into your meetings by repeat-
ing important phrases and varying your intonations. Similarly, tone
is how we express emotion audibly. Your tone should match your
message. And when it doesn't, that's a clue. As a manager, listen for
team members' tone changing during calls. Are you picking up on
sadness, stress, or frustration? However, this is just one signal. As
Cat explained, it can be challenging for some employees to pick up
on these subtle auditory cues.

3. Pause

A pause can be *so* . . . powerful. It can be used as a verbal punctu-
ation mark or a moment for everyone to reflect on your statement.
Sometimes you'll want to use a pause as a cue that others can chime
in with comments or questions. In that scenario, make your pause
longer to allow time for folks to unmute.

4. Eye Contact and Body Language

Eye contact and hand gestures are the foundations of nonverbal
communication. However, they look different on video calls. You'll
want to look directly at the camera at shoulder height to mimic eye
contact and quickly glance at the other attendees to check for understanding. Camera angles can trigger power dynamics. Looking down
at the other participants can suggest the same thing figuratively.

5. Creating Interactions

This last hack is all about the other person. How can you get them involved in the meeting? You'll want to design moments for interaction—whether that's a simple open-ended question or features like polls, breakout rooms, or the whiteboard.

For example, when Tam was a designer at IDEO during the COVID-19 pandemic, she and her team tried to re-create the magic of the IDEO office by designing a 3D experience in Figma. They led the client virtually through a reproduction of a museum filled with framed paintings that represented research insights and design concepts. This playful experience took the client away from their 13-inch screen box and into a playful experience for more engagement.

If you decide that a meeting is worth your collective time, encourage everyone to play a role. Ken Weary of Hotjar suggests the 10 percent rule: "Every participant in the meeting should be expected to contribute by speaking at least 10 percent of the time. If you're not speaking at least 10 percent of the time, you shouldn't be in the meeting, and therefore you should politely decline."

🔍 SPOTLIGHT STORY: Creating Virtual Engagement

According to Jason Morwick, the first time he transitioned his 40-hour Six Sigma course from in person to online at Cisco, "I thought people were going to come after me with pitchforks and torches. It was a miserable experience."

He'd made a common remote working mistake: copying and pasting what worked in person to video. But as you might guess, eight hours on Webex isn't exactly how people want to spend their time. Jason had to rethink the training from the ground up, and the next time he gave the training, he made the following changes:

- **Prework:** He shifted easy topics to asynchronous prework in the form of prerecorded videos and saved the tough stuff, like statistics, for the live training.

- **Interactivity:** He incorporated all of the tools within Webex, like annotations, polling, and chat windows, and invited an assistant trainer to monitor the chat.

- **Engagement:** Even though the content was in 2.5-hour modules, according to Jason, "You have seven minutes until they are asleep. Every seven minutes, I ask them a question to answer in chat or ask them to take a poll. They have to interact with the screen in some way."

Jason knew he'd reached the promised land when a student told him, "This course was more interactive and more engaging over Webex than if we were in person."

By making a few changes that encouraged user participation and asynchronous communication, Jason unlocked the power of the live, virtual meeting.

Practical Tips for Creating Interaction

Here are a few tools and methods that we learned about in our expert interviews to enhance meetings. Plus, they offer a new element of equity and democratization:

- **Dory:** Anyone can submit a question for an all-hands, and folks can up-vote/down-vote specific questions. It also enables the presenter to answer unaddressed questions asynchronously afterward.

- **Pulse:** Individuals can vote 1 through 5 on how they are feeling. This could be personally, professionally, or about a project or a strategic decision. It's a great way to quickly take a pulse on the general sentiment.

- **Facilitators:** You can rotate key positions: facilitator, time-keeper, and notetaker. This ensures that everyone is invested and can bring their unique flavor to the meeting.

- **Stacks:** Rather than the loudest and more confident people monopolizing the meeting, have people type "stack" into the chat window of whatever platform you are using. When it's time for questions, the facilitator can go through the stacks in order.

- **Breaks:** Not everyone can sit still for 90 minutes at a time. Giving people five or 10 minutes to stretch or grab food can reenergize the group. You can also do micro breaks together by turning on music and standing up for portions of the call—allowing people who do not need a physical break to socially connect.

- **Closed captions:** We often consider time zones for remote meetings, but it's also important to remember that colleagues may not speak the same first language or might have language-processing issues. Cat Contillo, who is autistic and has auditory processing issues, told us that it can be difficult for her to follow along with verbal-only communication. She relies heavily on closed captions and transcripts using Otter.ai, which helps her avoid getting lost.

❓ REFLECTION QUESTIONS

1. What could be your hero hack (something you are naturally talented at) for synchronous meetings?

2. Which of the Five Hacks for great video meetings were the most challenging? How can you practice in your next meeting?

CIRCLING BACK: TEAM COMMUNICATION ASSESSMENT (TAKE TWO)

Yes, we know. Another table! But you already have a head start. Remember that Team Communication Assessment you worked through at the beginning of the chapter?

Knowing what you know now—in light of the ABCs (asynchronous before calls) and your meeting audit—how would you adjust the way your team communicates? This is your chance to "circle back" (get it?) and make changes (table 8.5).

Ultimately, the ABC of remote communication comes down to two things: intentionality and discernment. Why should something be a meeting when it can be an email? How can you up your communication game with OALYWEN and the Five Hacks? Remember, it's about *better* communication, not more communication!

TABLE 8.5 RW Team Communication Assessment—Circling Back

COMMUNICATION EVENT	ORIGINAL FORMAT (CIRCLE ONE)	NEW FORMAT (USING THE ABCS)	RATIONALE FOR THE CHANGE
One-way communication			
Team announcements	Async // Sync		
Personal updates	Async // Sync		
Status updates	Async // Sync		
Two-way communication			
Brainstorming and collaboration	Async // Sync		
Ad-hoc questions	Async // Sync		
Relationship building	Async // Sync		
Conflict resolution	Async // Sync		
Performance feedback	Async // Sync		

(continued)

Project-based communication			
Project coordination and planning	Async // Sync .		
Project kickoffs	Async // Sync		
Project feedback and iteration	Async // Sync		
Add your own . . .			
. . . .	Async // Sync		
. . . .	Async // Sync		

♀ ALI'S ADVICE

Bottom line: if you are going to ask for someone's time, be respectful of it. We already discussed the basics, like having an agenda, but also think about the *times* when you meet.

There needs to be a shift from "business hours" meeting times to "most respectful meeting times." If you are based in New York, and your two other team members are in Ho Chi Minh City, Vietnam, and Chicago, setting business hours as 9 to 5 p.m. Eastern time is inconsiderate for the person based in Vietnam. Tools like the World Clock Meeting Planner can help you find a time that works for everyone—for example, 7 a.m. Central time for Chicago, 8 a.m. Eastern time for New York, and 8 p.m. GMT+7 for Ho Chi Minh City. Also, remember energy tracking! Some people may have a preference for early mornings or late nights.

The same can be true for team-building and social events. Try to include them as part of your regular meetings rather than scheduling an additional meeting. This respects work-life boundaries and makes bonding a normal part of business activity.

☺ TAM'S TIPS

My biggest challenge with asynchronous communication isn't the communication part itself. It's waiting—especially if there was an underlying disagreement or difference of opinion. I can still remember walking along the river in Belgrade or the moonlit sea of Malta as a digital nomad with my mind in a different place. Instead of admiring the sunset or the architecture, I kept wondering if the other person had read my message. And if so, did they understand? Why were they being so difficult!

That was when my coach, Akshay, introduced me to a quote by Viktor Frankl: "Between stimulus and response, there is a space. In that space is our power to choose our response. In our response lies our growth and our freedom."

There's a limit to what I can control at work. After I've responded to a sensitive situation, it's not fruitful to keep reacting to the situation by replaying it over and over again in my mind. This is a practice—and definitely does not happen overnight—but little by little, I found I could enjoy the sunset more and think about Slack conversations less.

CONCLUSION

WE'VE COME A LONG WAY! Since we aren't there to celebrate with you IRL, please pat yourself on the back, give yourself a high-five, and then turn up the music and dance. You deserve it!

Not only have you made it through a myriad of elaborate metaphors and puns, but you've worked through the foundations for becoming a *great* remote work manager in all of its forms.

Think of this as a movie montage for a moment, as we remind you of the greatest hits from *Remote Works*.

You've learned that people management is only one way of showing up as a manager within your organization. And that you were likely remote working before you knew it had a name—whether sending emails on a business trip or from your desk. You've assessed the Who, What, When, Where, Why, and How of what's shifted and, more important, how to leverage that shift and approach work from a remote state of mind.

Regardless of your musical abilities, you now have a Manager Archetype that places you in the same league as Beethoven and Maceo Parker. You've seen how you can stand on the shoulders of giants, applying motivation theory to managing your team. Remember, even you, as the manager, still need security, autonomy, mastery, and connection.

You've learned that conflict is natural, that your team will storm, but you have the tools to navigate your team through choppy waters to the land of performing with the RW Team Charter in hand. You can visualize and build a Digital House for your team and know what goes where, and while it sounds like a riddle, you know that not all time is created equal. So, manage your energy, not your time.

If you feel overwhelmed, you can lean on the RW Blueprint to add accountability, ownership, and structure to your workflow. Lastly, you know that a meeting is only one way of communicating at work. So audit that calendar and move more to asynchronous channels. It's the only way to truly unlock full autonomy at work.

OK, that's the end montage (but wasn't that fun?).

We're excited not only for you but for all the people you interact with daily. We believe that you will be the spark, the catalyst, and the role model in your organization. You can teach others that the status quo is just that: the bare minimum, the baseline, basic. It is OK to dream bigger, want more, and question assumptions like "Why do we work in this office?" and "Why are we having this meeting?" Remember, once you question one thing, you can ask everything. That is the essence of the future of work.

We've covered a lot, and we want to remind you that you're building a muscle. It's not always going to be easy. There will be pushback. There will be experiments that fail and communication that you wish had gone differently. But day by day, you're getting stronger at working remotely, which matters.

Why? Because designing your remote work life can *literally change* your life. You get to choose how, where, and when to get your work done in a way that's personalized and customized to you—whether that's popping around different cafés and different countries like Ali or furiously writing at midnight like Tam, our night owl.

We both firmly believe that remote work has fundamentally changed all aspects of our lives, from where we live, to how we work, to whom we've partnered with, to how we manage stress, health, and all the beautiful things that make life worth living. We wouldn't be the people we are today or surrounded by the people we call our community, both near and far, personal and professional, without remote work.

As Seneca once said, "It is not that we have a short space of time, but that we waste much of it."[1] How will you use your time? Ultimately, that is your life. What does a good life look like *for you*?

No pressure (OK, just a little bit, the healthy kind). We believe in you. You've got this!

To your best remote work life,

Ali & Tam

Remote Works
Discussion Guide

RW JOURNEYS

Welcome to RW Journeys! This guide contains everything you need to experience the principles of *Remote Works* as a group. RW Journeys can meet anywhere—from your local coworking spot, an office space, or that cozy coffee shop you love, or in a videoconference.

While anyone can form an RW Journeys group, we highly recommend it for learning and development, HR, and people ops teams as an alternative to formal management training for your company. Within self-directed groups, employees can learn how to make remote actually work within your organization.

The Approach

RW Journeys are an invitation to find a remote working community and solve remote work challenges together. There is no one way to do remote work. It's all about experimentation and finding what works for you and your team.

The Groups

We recommend between four and six members in a Journey group with a designated facilitator. You may want to group people based on their managerial role (e.g., people manager, project manager) or functional expertise (e.g., accounting, sales, engineering) to enhance the group dynamics. Don't forget to include those aspiring to manage as well!

The Cadence

Here are some ways to divide the chapters depending on the length of your desired journey:

- **The Sprint:** Two months (meet weekly—one chapter per week)

- **Short-Haul Journey:** Four months (meet biweekly—two chapters per month)

- **Long-Haul Journey:** Eight months (meet monthly—one chapter per month)

The Ground Rules

- Sharing works only when people feel psychologically safe within the group. Therefore, all RW Journey groups should commit to the three Cs:

- **Confidentiality:** I will keep whatever is shared in the Journey group confidential.

- **Communication:** I will listen deeply and communicate openly and honestly.

- **Commitment:** I will come to the monthly meetings fully present and prepared. I will contact the facilitator ahead of time if I cannot attend.

Deep Listening and Lived Practice

RW Journey groups practice deep listening, inspired by Quaker sitting circles. Each member listens quietly as they share their reflections on the *Remote Works* chapter. The facilitator will then open the floor for members to reflect on each other's insights. The facilitator ensures that everyone feels included and prevents crosstalk.

RW Journey groups are more than a book club. Using the prompts and reflections shared within the group, members should pick one activity they can test to put what they are learning into practice.

The Meeting Flow

Before the Meeting

- Members will read the assigned chapters.

- Members will pick one reflection question or excerpt from the chapter that stood out to them and contemplate how it applies to their work life.

- Members will brainstorm one experiment they can try based on the reading.

At the Meeting

Meetings usually last an hour, though you can lengthen as needed, and follow this format:

- **Opening (5 minutes):** The facilitator starts the meeting with a reminder of the themes covered in the *Remote Works* chapters for the month, leaning on the TL;DRs at the beginning of each chapter.

- **Personal Pulse Check (5 minutes):** The facilitator leads the members in a brief check-in to see how members are feeling.

The members can then use the same format with their teams at work. Here are two potential formats:

○ **Traffic Lights:** Use the colors green (good), yellow (meh), and red (mayday!) to describe how you're doing today.

○ **Rose, Thorn, Bud:** Describe a positive thing that happened (a rose), a negative thing that happened (a thorn), and something you're looking forward to (a bud).

- **Lived Practice (10 minutes):** Members share how last month's lived practice went and discuss any open questions before continuing the journey to the next chapter.

- **Reflecting (15 minutes):** The facilitator asks members to share a reflection question or chapter concept that challenges them and how they might integrate the learnings into their daily lives. Each member has about three minutes to share, while the rest of the Journey group listens. Once the member has finished speaking, they can call on the next person to share.

- **Responding (10 minutes):** After everyone has had a chance to share, the facilitator opens up the floor for members to comment on others' reflections and listen to lessons learned. This is an opportunity for members to gain insights from each other.

- **Commitments (10 minutes):** Members choose a concrete action they can practice with before the next meeting.

- **Closing Words (5 minutes):** The facilitator shares the concrete actions at the end of the meeting and through a follow-up email for accountability. They close the meeting with a reminder of the chapter for next month.

RW STUDENT CASE STUDY

Take a moment and imagine your top-choice employer after graduation. Maybe it's a nonprofit with a mission statement that gives you goosebumps. Or a CPG (consumer product goods) company that makes the world's best veggie burger.

Whatever it is, guess what—not only did you land an internship at The World's Best Company (TWBC), but they've asked you to come back next summer—except this time, they want you to design the internship program.

The Ask

TWBC has embraced a "remote state of mind" and has recruited 100 undergrads for their upcoming eight-week remote internship program. Interns will be evaluated on their performance at the end of the internship and offered full-time employment if successful.

TWBC management has laid out a few goals for the remote internship program:

- **The Work:** Interns need to take on real work whenever possible to understand what a full-time job would entail.

- **The Culture:** Interns should get a feel for TWBC's internal culture, mission, and goals.

- **The People:** Interns should participate in networking and social events, not only with each other but with senior employees.

The Deliverable

Luckily, you've read *Remote Works* and are up for the design challenge. There are four deliverables that you've been asked to design.

1. **Intern User Guides:** Everyone at TWBC is excited to meet the
    new interns, and all the interns, of course, are eager to meet
    each other. Using the RW User Guide template from chapter 3,
    develop a User Guide questionnaire to send to upcoming interns
    to learn more about them and their working styles. TWBC will
    then collate this information and share it with the rest of the
    organization.

2. **Collaboration Kickoff:** You know what it's like to be an
    intern—all the excitement and the fears. Now, it's time for
    you to put your firsthand experience into practice. Using the
    RW Collaboration Kickoff template from chapter 3, develop a
    conversation guide for managers to onboard interns. Feel free to
    adjust the prompts to make them relevant to college students.

3. **Intern Digital House:** It can be overwhelming to join a new
    company, especially as an intern. Therefore, you've been asked
    to create an online portal that will orient interns to the com-
    pany's inner workings. Create a brief that outlines what should
    be on the landing page of the online portal for interns. Refer to
    chapter 5 to see what types of tools and information that interns
    may need during their internship.

4. **One Social Event:** Although remote, TWBC still meets together
    in person a few times per year. However, since interns are at
    TWBC for only eight weeks, they will not get a chance to meet
    in person. You've been tasked to plan one event, either asyn-
    chronously or synchronously, that's purely social for interns. Put
    together a plan and schedule for the event, and describe why you
    believe it will create a bonding moment across the intern class.
    Refer to chapters 4 and 8 for thought starters. Remember, you
    can break the internship class into small groups, send physical
    items in the mail, or incorporate online games or activities.

Things to Note

- You get to decide which company will be the TWBC. Use this as a chance to research companies you're interested in, and use public information to customize the deliverables.

- Remember, you and your peers are the target audience. Tailor the deliverable to what college interns want to know and learn from an internship experience. Feel free to integrate technology and tools that interns might be more familiar with (e.g., YouTube videos, TikTok).

- Be creative and think outside the box! Feel free to experiment with tools like MURAL, Canva, or even WordPress, to mock up deliverables rather than just writing about them.

- Have fun! Remote work is new territory. How can you help interns embrace the remote state of mind? Refer to chapter 1 for inspiration.

Experts

MEET OUR FEATURED remote experts. Interviews were conducted by Ali Greene and Tamara Sanderson live and asynchronously between May 7, 2021, and May 15, 2022.

The following is a list of everyone who was interviewed and featured in the making of *Remote Works*, including their roles and organizations, as of May 15, 2022:

> Julie Armendariz, Senior HR Partner, HubSpot; previous HR/leader roles at Cisco Systems, Capital One, and GitLab
>
> Mario Giulio Bertorelli, Cofounder, Atium.app
>
> Darcy Boles, Remote Work Consultant, Culture Architect, and Experience Designer
>
> Ali Brandt, Product Leader and Owner, Ali Brandt Consulting; experience at Mahana Therapeutics, Gusto, Gojek, Change.org, and Kiva.org
>
> Ben Brooks, Founder and CEO, PILOT (employee coaching software product)

Hilary Callaghan, Founder, HRebel, and Senior Technical Recruiter, Canva

Lorraine Charles, Cofounder, Na'amal

Bill Connor, Talent Acquisition Manager, DuckDuckGo

Cat Contillo, ThreatOps Analyst, Huntress

Daniel Davis, Former Communications Manager, DuckDuckGo

Phil Freo, VP Product and Engineering, Close.com

Noah Gale, Cofounder, Tribe AI

Andrew Gobran, People Operations Generalist, Doist

Shuhan He, MD, Instructor of Medicine, Harvard Medical School

Taylor Jacobson, Founder and CEO, Focusmate

Cody Jones, Global Head of Partnerships and Channels, Zapier

Akshay Kapur, Head of Coaching, Automattic

Staszek Kolarzowski, Cofounder, Pilot (payroll, compliance, and benefits for remote teams)

Rachel Korb, Head of People and Culture, Uizard

Anne McCarthy, Developer Relations Wrangler, Automattic

Siobhan McKeown, COO, Human Made

Mike McNair, Vice President–Aerospace, SAE Industry Technologies Consortia; previously at L-3 Communications

Jason Morwick, Head of Remote-First, Cactus Communications; previously at Cisco Systems

Zbigniew Motak, Director of Talent Acquisition, DuckDuckGo

Jaclyn Rice Nelson, Cofounder, Tribe AI

Sara Robertson, Project Manager, University of Edinburgh, Futures Institute

Carlos Silva, Senior Content Writer, Semrush

Sally Thornton, CEO and Founder, Forshay Consulting

Nick Valluri, formerly held senior partnership roles at Coda and Zapier

Laïla von Alvensleben, Head of Culture and Collaboration, MURAL

Chase Warrington, Head of Remote, Doist

Ken Weary, COO, Hotjar

Steph Yiu, Chief Customer Officer, WordPress VIP (owned by Automattic)

Sahar Yousef, PhD, Cognitive Neuroscientist and Faculty, UC Berkeley Haas School of Business

Notes

Introduction

1. *Office Space* is a 1999 American satire of typical mid-to-late-1990s work life, starring Ron Livingston and Jennifer Aniston.

2. People Operations is a functional group that includes HR, company culture, and employee engagement.

3. E. E. Cummings, *E. E. Cummings: A Miscellany Revised* (New York: October House, 1965).

Chapter 1

1. Woody Leonhard, *Underground Guide to Telecommuting* (Boston, MA: Addison-Wesley, 1995).

2. Annamarie Mann, "Why We Need Best Friends at Work," Gallup.com, January 15, 2018.

3. Prithwiraj (Raj) Choudhury, "Our Work-from-Anywhere Future," *Harvard Business Review*, November–December 2020, https://hbr.org/2020/11/our-work-from-anywhere-future.

4. "Listicle" is an article based around a list.

5. Matt Mullenweg, "Distributed Work's Five Levels of Autonomy," Matt Mullenweg, April 10, 2020, https://ma.tt/2020/04/five-levels-of-autonomy/.

Chapter 2

1. Coleman Barks, *The Essential Rumi* (New York: HarperOne, 2004), 252.

2. C. G. Jung, *The Undiscovered Self* (Princeton, NJ: Princeton University Press, 1990).

3. Daniel Goleman, "Leadership That Gets Results," *Harvard Business Review*, March–April 2000.

4. Yes, that is a pun for Ed Sheeran, the famous British pop singer who is most famous for his 2017 song "Shape of You," and Led Zeppelin, the English rock band formed in the late 1960s.

Chapter 3

1. We recommend a synchronous meeting unless your team is performing at level four or five on the Five Levels of Autonomy.

Chapter 4

1. Jackie MacMullan, Rafe Bartholomew, and Dan Klores, "'What did we just watch?' The bronze that broke USA Basketball," ESPN, August 30, 2019, https://www.espn.com/nba/story/_/id/27462338/what-did-just-watch -bronze-broke-usa-basketball.

2. Patrick M. Lencioni, *The Five Dysfunctions of a Team: A Leadership Fable*, J-B Lencioni Series (London, UK: Jossey-Bass, 2002).

3. Bruce W. Tuckman, "Developmental Sequence in Small Groups," *Psychological Bulletin* 63, no. 6 (1965): 384–99.

4. Bruce W. Tuckman and Mary Ann C. Jensen, "Stages of Small Group Development Revisited," *Group and Organization Studies* 2, no. 4 (1977): 419–27.

5. A type of organizational structure where a person reports to two or more leaders.

6. Jason Fried, "How We Structure Our Work and Teams at Basecamp," *Signal v. Noise*, November 17, 2016, https://m.signalvnoise.com/how-we-structure- our-work-and-teams-at-basecamp/.

7. You can pull from the RW Team Mission Statement here. For functional- based teams with isolated workflows, expand the definition of success away from individual work. Make the goals more about how you can support each other in the reasons *why* your team exists.

8. Tim Bontemps, "Born from the Fires of 2004 Failures, Team USA Basketball Now Built to Last," *Chicago Tribune*, July 21, 2016, https://www .chicagotribune.com/sports/olympics/ct-usa-basketball-built-to-last -20160721-story.html.

Chapter 5

1. USA Memory Championship, About, https://www.usamemorychampionship .com/about/.

2. Molly Talbert, "How Work about Work Gets in the Way of Real Work," Asana, March 21, 2020, https://asana.com/resources/why-work-about -work-is-bad.

3. "Dogfooding" means using your own product or service.

Chapter 6

1. Susie Cranston and Scott Keller, "Increasing the 'Meaning Quotient' of Work," *McKinsey Quarterly*, January 1, 2013, https://www.mckinsey.com /business-functions/people-and-organizational-performance/our-insights /increasing-the-meaning-quotient-of-work.

2. "Becoming Superhuman," https://www.becomingsuperhuman.science/.

3. Sahar Yousef, PhD, *The Science of Productivity and Performance in Our Busy, Always-On World*, https://hr.berkeley.edu/sites/default/files/science_of_wfh _productivity_and_well-being_-_now_conference.pdf.

4. Annie Dillard, *The Writing Life* (New York: Harper Perennial, 2013).

5. Tim Urban, "100 Blocks a Day," October 21, 2016, https://waitbutwhy .com/2016/10/100-blocks-day.html.

6. Shishir Mehrotra, "The Color-What-Matters Calendar Guide," Coda.io, https://coda.io/@shishir/color-what-matters-calendar.

Chapter 8

1. *Wah-wah* is the noise of a sad trombone; you can also interchange it with *boo-hoo*, like a kid crying.

2. Julia Sklar, "'Zoom Fatigue' Is Taxing the Brain. Here's Why That Happens," *National Geographic*, April 24, 2020, https://www.nationalgeographic.com /science/article/coronavirus-zoom-fatigue-is-taxing-the-brain-here-is-why -that-happens.

3. Susan Weinschenk, *100 Things Every Designer Needs to Know About People* (Berkeley, CA: New Riders, 2011), 68–69.

4. Vinh Giang, https://www.vinhgiang.com/.

Conclusion

1. Seneca, *On the Shortness of Life: Life Is Long if You Know How to Use It*, trans. C. D. N. Costa (New York: Penguin Books, 2005).

Glossary

Asana: Project management tool to help teams manage their work, projects, and tasks online.

Async: Internal communication tool developed and used by Zapier.

Atium: Online app featuring a library of games and activities designed for remote relationship building. Atium was named the "Hottest Remote Work Startup" by Running Remote in August 2020.

Automattic: Parent company of WordPress.com, along with a suite of related tools and products, like WooCommerce, Jetpack, Tumblr, WordPress VIP, and more. Remote since inception in 2005.

Basecamp: Project management tool developed by remote work advocates Jason Fried and David Heinemeier Hansson.

Becoming Superhuman: Productivity lab led by Sahar Yousef, PhD, a cognitive neuroscientist and lecturer at UC Berkeley's Haas School of Business.

Canva: Online graphic design tool.

Cactus Communications: Online translation service for scientific research.

Close.com: Customer relationship management software.

Coda: Web-based document platform with word-processing, spreadsheet, and presentation capabilities. Often used to create an internal wiki.

Copper CRM: Customer relationship management software.

Desana: On-demand workspaces app.

Discord: A VoIP and instant messaging social platform.

Doist: Fully remote company since 2007 specializing in productivity software, namely Todoist (productivity software) and Twist (asynchronous messaging).

DuckDuckGo: Privacy-based search engine with browser extension and mobile app. Remote-first since inception in 2008.

Edinburgh Futures Institute: Future-thinking lab at the University of Edinburgh.

Figma: Collaborative graphics editor and prototyping tool.

Focusmate: Virtual coworking service and community.

Forshay Consulting: Executive search and interim placement service with a focus on diversity.

GitHub: Internet hosting for software development and version control using Git. Owned by Microsoft.

GitLab: Open-source platform for developers to manage source code; famous for its transparent remote work practices.

Google Workspace (formerly G-Suite and Google Hangouts): Suite of collaboration tools such as Gmail, Calendar, Drive, Docs, and Google Meet.

Hotjar: Website visualization tool to understand user behavior.

HRebel: Recruitment, hiring, and people and culture consultancy.

HubSpot: Customer relationship management software with marketing, sales, content, and customer service features.

Human Made: WordPress development and digital experiences agency.

Huntress: Cybersecurity platform.

IDEO: Design and innovation firm known for design thinking.

Jira: Software development and project management tool owned by Atlassian.

Krisp: Software to eliminate background noises for online meetings; https://krisp.ai/.

L-3 Communications: Supplier of command and control, communication, and avionics products.

LinkedIn: Professional social networking site.

Looker: Business intelligence platform to support data analytics.

Loom: Asynchronous video communication tool to send short videos and screen recordings.

Meetup: Platform for finding and building local communities.

Mentimeter: Interactive presentation tool with polls, quizzes, and word clouds.

Microsoft Teams: Workspace chat and videoconferencing platform.

Monday: Project management tool used to help teams manage their work, projects, and tasks online.

Miro: Online whiteboard and collaboration tool.

MURAL: Online whiteboard and collaboration tool.

Na'amal: Training and remote job placement for refugees.

Notion: Web-based document platform with word-processing, spreadsheet, and presentation capabilities. Often used to create an internal wiki.

Oyster: Employment platform for hiring and providing benefits to employees and contractors worldwide.

P2: Internal WordPress-powered blogging system at Automattic.

Photoshop: Photo-editing software from Adobe.

PILOT: Employee-development platform founded by Ben Brooks.

Pilot: Payroll, compliance, and benefits platform for remote teams, cofounded by Staszek Kolarzowski.

Prezi: Online software for creating visual presentations.

SAE Industry Technologies Consortia: Association for public and private organizations to collaborate on standards and best practices in the aerospace industry.

Salesforce: Customer relationship management software.

Slack: Cloud-based messaging platform designed for workplaces, owned by Salesforce.

Tumblr: Micro-blogging platform, acquired by Automattic from Verizon in 2019.

Trello: Task-management tool known for Kanban-style lists, owned by Atlassian.

Uizard: Online AI-powered design tool for creating mobile and web mock-ups.

WhatsApp: Internet-based text messaging app, owned by Meta.

Whereby: Videoconferencing tool.

WolframAlpha: Computational knowledge and answer engine developed with remote CEO.

WordPress VIP: Agile content platform for enterprise organizations, owned by Automattic.

World Clock Meeting Planner: Website for planning meetings according to time zones; https://www.timeanddate.com/worldclock/meeting.html.

Yac: Asynchronous voice message and screen share application.

Zapier: Platform to easily integrate apps and automate workflows.

Zendesk: Online customer support management tool.

Zoom: Videoconferencing tool.

Acknowledgments

TO EVERYONE WHO KNOWS, deep down, that work can be better, thank you.

It takes a village to write a book and, in this case, a very engaging virtual village. We could never have written *Remote Works* without the support, encouragement, and wisdom of so many along the way. We'd like to give a special thanks . . .

To our 34 remote work experts: You made this book happen. We are in awe of you and the work you and your companies do. Whether remote for years or quickly embracing change during the pandemic, you are the people we believe others should look up to when seeking best-in-class examples for working and leading remotely. We've learned so much from you and are grateful for your time, energy, and transparency during our interviews. We hope that your stories inspire the next generation of remote workers.

A special shout-out to Steph for finding Tam's résumé in the slush stack at Automattic; to Akshay for letting Tam turn the tables and have him do the talking for a change; to Ali Brandt for inspiring Tam to take the plunge into self-employment; to Ken for being the nomad family inspiration that Ali's always admired; to Chase for getting back to us on every one of those super-long email threads; to Andrew for sharing not only remote work tips but movie suggestions as well; to Sara, Darcy, Hilary, Laïla, and Sally for your vibe—our conversations were a breath of fresh air.

To our team at Berrett-Koehler: You've been an absolute dream to work with: Neal, for truly enjoyable and energizing collaboration sessions; Jeevan, we know it's you who makes everything work behind the scenes; Ashley, for pushing edges with our nontraditional approach to a business book cover. We are so happy you get us.

To our agents, Kim Peticolas and Maryann Karinch: Thanks for betting on us and finding us a publishing home.

To Matt Mullenweg: You've been such an inspiration to us and to workers around the world challenging the status quo of work. Thank you for putting your vision and ideas into practice at Automattic.

To Laurel Farrer, Tony Jamous, Karen Mangia, and Amy C. Edmondson: Thank you for your kind words and backing. It means a lot to us.

To Dale and Spencer: We never would have met without you and Hackers Paradise Cape Town.

To Marcos and Elisa: For that early introduction on Slack.

To Gabriella: For editing our very first book proposal. (It worked!)

• • • • • •

And given that there are two of us, a few personal shout-outs.

Ali's Shout-Outs

To Mom and Dad: Thanks for supporting my "weird" nomad dreams early on, even when it meant having me as an adult roommate the first time I quit my job to go backpacking. Thank you for always telling me (and others) how proud you are of me.

To Mike: Thanks for showing me in your short time what it means to live a full life.

To Heather: We are two different sides of the same coin. Thank you for living your mission to make physical workspaces beautiful. I am still waiting for our live debate. I love you for calling me out when I am being too "Ali" but knowing I always have your unconditional support!

To Tracy: My sister in spirit, cousin in reality, friend, and mentor in life. Thank you for your influence, advice, and generosity, and for coming to visit me in so many different places.

Zbig, Bill, Kristina, Mike, and my extended DuckDuckGo teammates: Thank you for letting me be the cheesy manager we all know I *really* am. You are some of the best coworkers I could have ever asked for!

Finally, JP: Thanks for putting me in the hot seat and challenging me to grow as a person. You knew I had something to share with the world before I did. I laughed when you told me I should write my thoughts down, and yet here we are! Thank you for making me coffee every morning, for having a signature dish to cook when I am feeling stressed, for always knowing how to make me laugh, and for believing in me. I love you.

Tam's Shout-Outs

To my parents: For your early encouragement of my writing (remember that Xanga blog?) and reading the first draft of *Remote Works*. Thank you for always being my biggest fans and two of my favorite travel companions!

To Akshay: For your coaching and mentorship. You've helped me listen to that still, quiet voice inside.

To Dr. Petty: For advising my college thesis and showing me early on that you can approach business with heart.

To Jess: For your lifelong friendship (despite my many moves) and your limitless hospitality whenever I'm back in San Francisco. Can't wait to see you soon!

To Mike: Who knew our long phone calls during the pandemic would change our lives? Thank you for encouraging me to write about remote work. (I took your advice!)

To Kirk: Thank you for helping me believe in myself and see the bigger picture in my work. Plus, you make an excellent cup of coffee.

Index

Please note that italicized page numbers followed by a *t* indicate tables, and those followed by an *f* indicate figures.

About the Authors

ALI GREENE AND TAMARA (TAM) SANDERSON are the cofounders of Remote Works, an organizational design and consulting firm with a mission to liberate teams from the nine-to-five and teach them how to do their best work, anytime, anywhere.

The pair have spent a combined nearly two decades in distributed environments, Ali as the former director of People Operations at DuckDuckGo and Tam as the director of strategic partnerships and corporate development at Automattic.

The duo believes that remote work skills are a requirement for managers and teams regardless of where (or what) their "office" looks like. In *Remote Works*, they share their firsthand experiences, interactive best practices, and lessons learned from dozens of expert interviews to make remote work *actually* work. To learn more about Ali and Tam, go to remoteworksbook.com.

ALI GREENE

In 2014, Ali shut the door on quintessential office life and opened the door to remote work. She didn't know what to expect on her journey, but she knew that commuting and office culture left her little time to explore her passions. So, she traded Madison Avenue for Machu Picchu.

Ali subsequently backpacked across South America, worked in bakeries in the United States, and supported companies *remotely* as an HR consultant—leaning on problem-solving skills she'd acquired at Undertone, LivingSocial, and Nike. ("Failing fast" applies just as readily to decorating a cake or missing a flight abroad as it does at a start-up.)

Her remote work expertise matured when she was director of People Operations for DuckDuckGo, where she supported building their fully distributed team from 30 to nearly 100. Most recently, Ali was the former head of culture and community at Oyster. Her dedication to "The Future of Work" has been recognized in the 2022 *Remote Influencer Report* by Remote.

Looking back, Ali recalls a few moments that made her look at life (and work!) differently: switching grade schools taught her how to adapt; losing a family member taught her to appreciate life and have fun; living as a digital nomad taught her the beauty of new perspectives and cultures.

Ali is passionate about nontraditional career flexibility and developing meaningful communities. (She's organized retreats in Mexico, Serbia, and France.) Outside of the "office," Ali loves hiking, board games, and experimenting with new recipes in the kitchen.

As she often says, "Working remotely allows us to do the things that work for us. You can manage work around your lifestyle, instead of the opposite." If you wish to connect with Ali, find her on LinkedIn at linkedin.com/in/greeneali.

TAMARA (TAM) SANDERSON

A college-study-abroad flyer and subsequent internet searches lured Tamara to London nearly two decades ago. It was intended to be a four-month adventure, but sometimes life has different plans. That experience transformed her from someone who thought she'd never leave Texas to a traveler. She has spent nine years as an expat, visited 70 countries, and even sailed to Antarctica—all while working full-time.

Tamara was a remote worker before she knew it had a name. She began her career as a management consultant at Oliver Wyman (where she took any international project that came her way) and as a private equity analyst at Audax Group. Later, she cut her teeth on tech and design at Google, Automattic (WordPress.com), and IDEO.

Tamara is passionate about helping others find their paths. As Joseph Campbell once said, "If you can see your path laid out in front of you step-by-step, you know it's not your path. Your own path you make with every step you take. That's why it's your path."

While she's put up her suitcase for now, she's found new passionate projects: building a library in her 700-square-foot apartment, tending to a balcony garden, learning how to cook, making art, and getting involved in her local community.

Call her an idealist, but she truly believes that remote work can change the opportunity equation for people when they are able to fully embrace one another's autonomy, dignity, and ingenuity.

Tamara lives in Cambridge, Massachusetts, and is always looking for a coworking buddy. She can be found at tamarasanderson.com.

Berrett–Koehler
Publishers

Berrett-Koehler is an independent publisher dedicated to an ambitious mission: *Connecting people and ideas to create a world that works for all.*

Our publications span many formats, including print, digital, audio, and video. We also offer online resources, training, and gatherings. And we will continue expanding our products and services to advance our mission.

We believe that the solutions to the world's problems will come from all of us, working at all levels: in our society, in our organizations, and in our own lives. Our publications and resources offer pathways to creating a more just, equitable, and sustainable society. They help people make their organizations more humane, democratic, diverse, and effective (and we don't think there's any contradiction there). And they guide people in creating positive change in their own lives and aligning their personal practices with their aspirations for a better world.

And we strive to practice what we preach through what we call "The BK Way." At the core of this approach is *stewardship,* a deep sense of responsibility to administer the company for the benefit of all of our stakeholder groups, including authors, customers, employees, investors, service providers, sales partners, and the communities and environment around us. Everything we do is built around stewardship and our other core values of *quality, partnership, inclusion,* and *sustainability.*

This is why Berrett-Koehler is the first book publishing company to be both a B Corporation (a rigorous certification) and a benefit corporation (a for-profit legal status), which together require us to adhere to the highest standards for corporate, social, and environmental performance. And it is why we have instituted many pioneering practices (which you can learn about at www.bkconnection.com), including the Berrett-Koehler Constitution, the Bill of Rights and Responsibilities for BK Authors, and our unique Author Days.

We are grateful to our readers, authors, and other friends who are supporting our mission. We ask you to share with us examples of how BK publications and resources are making a difference in your lives, organizations, and communities at www.bkconnection.com/impact.

Dear reader,

Thank you for picking up this book and welcome to the worldwide BK community! You're joining a special group of people who have come together to create positive change in their lives, organizations, and communities.

What's BK all about?

Our mission is to connect people and ideas to create a world that works for all.

Why? Our communities, organizations, and lives get bogged down by old paradigms of self-interest, exclusion, hierarchy, and privilege. But we believe that can change. That's why we seek the leading experts on these challenges—and share their actionable ideas with you.

A welcome gift

To help you get started, we'd like to offer you a **free copy** of one of our bestselling ebooks:

www.bkconnection.com/welcome

When you claim your **free ebook**, you'll also be subscribed to our blog.

Our freshest insights

Access the best new tools and ideas for leaders at all levels on our blog at ideas.bkconnection.com.

Sincerely,

Your friends at Berrett-Koehler